The Case for Caribbean Reparatory Justice

The Case for Caribbean Reparatory Justice
©2014 Ralph E. Gonsalves

Printed in the United States

This is the second volume in a series entitled
Caribbean Ideas
published by Strategy Forum, Inc.
Kingstown, St. Vincent and the Grenadines

Other titles in the series include
Our Caribbean Civilisation and its Political Prospects

The Case for Caribbean Reparatory Justice

Four Essays by
Dr. The Hon. Ralph E. Gonsalves
Prime Minister of St. Vincent and the Grenadines

Table of Contents

Foreword   7

I. The End of Slavery in Saint Vincent   11
    and the Grenadines and
    Our Commemoration in 2012

II. Preliminary Notes on the Quantification   29
    of Reparation from the British for Lands Stolen,
    for Genocide and Forcible Deportation
    of the Garifuna People, and for Enslavement
    of Africans in St. Vincent and the Grenadines

III. A Review Essay of Hilary Beckles'   51
    Britain's Black Debt: Reparations for
    Caribbean Slavery and Native Genocide

IV. Road Map for Reparations for Native Genocide   89
    and Slavery in the Caribbean

Foreword

The General Assembly of the United Nations, through its resolution 68/237 of 23 December 2013, proclaimed the International Decade for People of African Descent scheduled to commence on 1 January 2015 and end on 31 December 2024. The International Decade for People of African Descent, with the theme "People of African Descent: Recognition, Justice and Development" will be launched on 10 December 2014, United Nations Human Rights Day, by a ceremony hosted by the President of the General Assembly. To mark the launch of this important historic Decade, this small collection of speeches and essays by the Prime Minister of Saint Vincent and the Grenadines, Dr. The Hon. Ralph E. Gonsalves, was compiled under the title "The Case for Caribbean Reparatory Justice". The collection begins with a statement made to the Saint Vincent and the Grenadines' Parliament on 31 July 2012 to commemorate "The End of Slavery in Saint Vincent and the Grenadines" and thus provides a Vincentian context for the broader discussion of Caribbean reparatory justice. The review essay of Sir Hilary Beckles' book entitled *Britain's Black Debt: Reparations for Caribbean Slavery and Native Genocide* forms the centrepiece of this small publication.

Dr. Gonsalves began his political activism in 1968 when, as President of the Guild of Undergraduates at the University of the West Indies, Mona, Jamaica, he led a massive protest of several thousand students and Jamaicans of all walks of life, but mainly from the working class, into the streets of capital Kingston to protest the government's banning of Dr. Walter Rodney, a Lecturer in History at the university, from re-entering Jamaica. Walter Rodney, an activist and revolutionary intellectual, Caribbean nationalist, socialist, and Black Power advocate, was a Guyanese national. Dr. Gonsalves, who is affectionately known as "The Comrade", has since become the voice of the victim. For instance, over the years, Dr. Gonsalves has vociferously advocated for the rights of Haitians. In September 2013, he stood before the United Nations General Assembly and boldly called upon the United Nations to acknowledge its responsibility for the recent cholera outbreak in Haiti. When the Dominican Republic decided to amend its laws retroactively denying birthright citizenship to Haitian-descended children, Prime Minister Gonsalves was again at the forefront defending those rights.

Today, Prime Minister Gonsalves is one of the leading voices and proponents in our Caribbean Community's quest for reparatory justice for slavery and the genocide of native peoples. On 15 September 2013, the Caribbean Community (CARICOM) opened the first Regional Reparations Conference in St. Vincent and the Grenadines. The Conference was mandated by the historic, unanimous decision of CARICOM Heads of Government in July 2013, in Trinidad and Tobago. The Heads of Government also requested each CARICOM Member State to set up its own National Reparations Committee to document the effects of European genocide against the indigenous inhabitants of the region, the slave trade in and the enslavement of Africans, and colonization. Not since the region's struggles for independence has the Caribbean embarked on a journey of such magnitude and importance for the future development of the people and region!

In January of this year, during the second Summit of the Community of Latin American and Caribbean States (CELAC), it was agreed in a Special Declaration on the issue of reparations that,

> ...slavery and the slave trade, including the transatlantic slave trade, were appalling tragedies in the history of humanity not only because of their abhorrent barbarism but also in terms of their magnitude, organized nature and especially their negation of the essence of the victims.

CELAC further declared slavery and the transatlantic slave trade to be "a crime against humanity" and recognized, "the enduring and nefarious legacy of native peoples, slavery and the plundering of resources and its impact on the conditions of underdevelopment in many countries of the region."

On 10 March 2014, at the 25th Inter-Sessional Meeting of the Conference of Heads of Government of CARICOM held in Saint Vincent and the Grenadines, the Heads adopted a 10-point action plan which now constitutes the basis for an elaboration of a Caribbean Reparatory Justice Programme and which, inter alia, includes requests for cultural institutions, an indigenous peoples development programme, psychological rehabilitation, and debt cancellation.

Prime Minister Gonsalves is of the view that the Caribbean must continue to advocate for reparatory justice in all international fora; that the quest for Caribbean reparatory justice must be a centerpiece of our region's foreign and domestic policies. The programme of activities to accompany the International Decade for People of African Descent calls on the international community, and international and regional organizations to "use the Decade as an opportunity to engage with people of African descent on appropriate and effective measures to halt and reverse the lasting consequences of slavery, the slave trade, the transatlantic slave trade in captured African people".

This small collection will contribute to the discussions as people of African descent join UN Member States, civil society and all relevant actors to contemplate issues related to "recognition, justice and development" for people of African descent during the Decade.

I. Rhonda King
November 2014

I.
The End Of Slavery in Saint Vincent and the Grenadines and Our Commemoration in 2012

Statement to Parliament on July 31, 2012

Background and Context

The Act for the Abolition of Slavery in the British Empire, of which St. Vincent and the Grenadines was part, was passed in the British Parliament in 1833. Emancipation Day was proclaimed to be August 01, 1834. An "apprenticeship" period followed; the slaves, who were transported through the horrendous Middle Passage from Africa, were finally and legally freed on August 1, 1838, 174 years ago.

In the year 1763, Britain assumed suzerainty over St. Vincent (renamed St. Vincent and the Grenadines since independence on October 27, 1979) in a general carve-up of the West Indies by the major European powers under the Treaty of Paris. Effective European settlement commenced henceforth. Save and except for a few years between the late 1770s and early 1780s when France had a temporary, tenuous colonial hold on St. Vincent, Britain remained the colonising power until our country attained internal self-government in 1969 and constitutional independence in 1979.

When Britain took colonial control in 1763, the population of St. Vincent consisted of approximately 10,000 (ten thousand) Kalinago and Garifuna, 1,380 French settlers and some 2,700 African slaves. The French were settled mainly on the western side of St. Vincent in occupation of under 2,000 acres of land: There were 114 parcels of land under the French which the British later converted into leaseholds, three of which were between 100 and 135 acres each; the other 111 parcels of land were under 100 acres each. All other lands, close to 100,000 acres, were held in common by the Kalinago and Garifuna people. Upon colonising St. Vincent, the British swiftly declared in 1764 that all the lands belonged to the British crown. Until 1800, the British systematically deprived the Kalinago and Garifuna people of their lands; the indigenous people (the Kalinago) and the Garifuna (the descendents of persons of mixed blood Kalinago and African) were pushed to the worst and most inhospitable parcels of land in the north-east of St. Vincent amounting to 238 acres.

The African component of the Garifuna people came from shipwrecked Africans in the late 17th century, runaway African slaves from Barbados, some African slaves who came by way of Martinique and Guadeloupe, and recent African slave arrivals under the British.

Late Colonial Settlement
of St. Vincent and the Grenadines

St. Vincent was settled much later than most of the other Caribbean territories because of the inhospitable terrain, the fierce defence of their patrimony by the Kalinago and Garifuna people, and their opposition to slavery. It is this much later settlement which accounted for the fact that African slavery as the dominant mode of socio-economic organisation emerged in St. Vincent only after the Kalinago and Garifuna (collectively called "Caribs" by the colonisers) were subdued and defeated in 1797 following the death of their Chief, Joseph Chatoyer, our National Hero. Colonies such as Jamaica, Barbados, St. Kitts, Cuba, and Hispaniola had long been settled by mercantile capitalism from Europe, utilising African slave labour on plantations. Slavery as a mode of production internal to

St. Vincent, predominantly on sugar-cane plantations, with capitalist exchange relations externally, emerged fully after 1800. In 1807 the slave trade came to an end; and slavery's abolition arrived in 1834.

Some relevant sugar production data are as follows: 1,930 tons in 1770; 2,049 tons in 1779, 35 tons in 1788; by far the most of which were exported. By 1807, sugar production had risen to 11,209 tons and steadied at 11,270 tons in 1814. Between 1820 and 1828, sugar production fluctuated in a range from 10,834 to 14,403 tons, the peak of 1828. The cataclysmic volcanic eruption of 1812, hurricanes of 1819 and 1830, and the vagaries of the international trade in sugar would have adversely affected sugar production.

The number of slaves increased correspondingly between 1763 and 1812 (1,300 in 1763; 5,000 slaves in 1798; and 24,920 in 1812) with the emergence and consolidation of sugar production. A decline in the number of slaves occurred closer to the date of emancipation: thus 22,997 slaves in 1832, and 18,794 in 1833, the last year before slavery ended. Joseph Spinelli explains the fall in numbers in his study, *Land Use and Population in St. Vincent 1763–1960* (Ph.D Dissertation, University of Florida, 1973), thus:

> The attrition in numbers of slaves was the result of the high mortality of an aging, predominantly male population without sufficient reproduction to compensate for deaths and periodic manumission of the elderly and infirm from the slave registers. It is evident from St. Vincent's court records of manumissions that the estate owners anticipated freedom for the black population and hastened the transition by releasing their less productive charges.

The bulk of the slaves were to be found in the Parishes of Charlotte and St. George on the eastern side of St. Vincent. The distribution by Parish for the year 1833 was as follows: Charlotte, 6,729 slaves; St. George, 4,994; St. Andrew, 1538; St. Patrick, 2,654; St. David, 1,519; and Bequia, 2,360.

As the nineteenth century unfolded in the post-emancipation years, the population of St. Vincent and the Grenadines was further augmented by "liberated" Africans, then by Portuguese indentured servants from Madeira, and a little later by indentured labourers from India. These three categories of arrivants numbered roughly 5,000 in the aggregate. Their descendants along with the off-spring of the Kalinago/Garifuna, the Anglo-Saxons, and Africans, and in their various creolised admixtures, make up today, alongside twentieth century migrants especially from the Middle East, the population of St. Vincent and the Grenadines which is still predominantly of African descent.

The End of Slavery

The "Act for the Abolition of Slavery" freed the slave children under six years of age from August 01, 1834. This Act had originally stipulated an apprenticeship period of six years for slaves classified as praedials (field hands), and four years for non-praedials (domestics, trades persons, and other non-field workers). However, the two-year differential between field slaves and non-field slaves was eventually dropped, and "the apprenticeship" for all ended on August 1, 1838.

Different sources provide varying numbers of slaves. The aforementioned comparative numbers for the various time-periods are sourced from *The Estate Book*. The authoritative figure for the Apprentice Population as at August 01, 1834, was 22,250, as provided by the "House of Commons: British Sessional Papers", 1835, volume 50. At page 685 thereof it is detailed that there were the following:

Praedial Attached	: 14,797
Praedial Unattached	: 512
Non-Praedial	: 2,793
Children under the age of six years	: 2,959
Aged, diseased or otherwise noneffective	: 1,189
Total	: 22,250

This figure closely approximates the number (22,997 slaves) for which there was the last year, before emancipation, of formal slave registration, 1832.

Consequent upon the passage of the "Act for the Abolition of Slavery throughout the British Colonies" in the Imperial Parliament of Great Britain and Ireland in 1833, there was passed in St. Vincent on April 02, 1834, a similar titled Act, namely: "An Act for the Abolition of Slavery in St. Vincent and its Dependencies, in consideration of Compensation, and for promoting the Industry and good conduct of the Manumitted Slaves". This act contained several preambles and 68 sections detailing the legislative and administrative arrangements for apprenticeship and emancipation. On September 09, 1835, the Lieutenant-Governor in St. Vincent, George Tyler, assented to a Bill passed on July 09, 1835, by both the Assembly and the Council, which repealed and amended certain provisions of the earlier Act of April 02, 1834. This later Act, containing 14 sections, was entitled "An Act to repeal certain Clauses, and to alter and amend an Act entitled 'An Act for the Abolition of Slavery in the Island of St. Vincent and its Dependencies, in consideration of Compensation, and for promoting the Industry and good conduct of the Manumitted Slaves'."

Apprenticeship Period

The four-year "apprenticeship" period, 1834 to 1838, is one demanding much more research since it signaled the commencement of an evolutionary struggle towards legal emancipation and, importantly, the shaping of post-emancipation society. One fascinating book of relevance to St. Vincent and the Grenadines in this regard is Professor Roderick A. Mc Donald's edited volume published in 2001 by the UWI Press and entitled, *Between Slavery and Freedom: Special Magistrate John Anderson's Journal of St. Vincent during the Apprenticeship*. John Anderson served as Special Magistrate at St. Vincent from January 1836 until his death in September 21, 1839, in Colonarie House. He was one of the Special Magistrates appointed to oversee the Apprenticeship period.

In the Introductory Essay to his edited volume, Professor Mc Donald tells us:

The Apprenticeship years did not ease the transition from slavery to freedom; instead, they ushered in a period of turmoil with which neither the British government's legislation nor its personnel could cope satisfactorily.

Anderson's Journal makes clear the jostling, struggles, contradictions, advances, setbacks, and compromises of the various contending forces in the society over a range of socio-economic matters by the praedials, non-praedials, free coloureds, creoles, Africans, the white planter-merchant class, the indigenous people, and the colonial officials.

Anderson, a pro-planter and colonial official, jaundiced in his views against black people, "Caribs", and workers, nevertheless had an observant eye for the forces at work.

Professor Mc Donald summarises all this, thus:

> Three factors labour assignment, colour, and ethnicity divided the apprentices. Anderson described the cleavages between praedials and non-praedials, blacks and coloureds, and Creoles and Africans, respectively: these categories, of course, overlapped considerably, since non-praedials, for example, were more likely to be coloured, and were almost invariably Creole. Moreover, in differentiating the terms of apprenticeship between agricultural and non-agricultural workers, the Emancipation Act had reinforced a division between field hands and domestics that dated from slavery, and through which some domestics from the group traditionally viewed by the planters and by themselves as an elite, apparently claimed superiority and derived status. Anderson documented a tendency among non-praedials to emulate free coloureds while distancing themselves from the praedial apprentices, which he suggested became more pronounced as the Apprenticeship neared its conclusion. Meanwhile he showed how domestics began to negotiate their relationship to their white employers by challenging the relations of power in ways that would have been much more problematic a few years earlier during slavery.

Most fascinating, perhaps, is the role and function of the bulk of the workers, "praedials" or field-hands. Roderick A. Mc Donald advises us:

> The praedials' strategies to achieve independence can be discerned in attitudes concerning the work required of them for their former owners, as well as their refusal to apprentice their children, and their determination to secure rights, and devote free time, to their homes, villages and provision grounds they had occupied since slavery, but over which the planters retained title. During the Apprenticeship, therefore, praedials concentrated on constructing the society they wanted to occupy in freedom: they wanted to minimize their involvement in the plantation system and base their post-emancipation world on the social and economic systems they had constructed in slavery. The houses, gardens and grounds where, as slaves, they had developed an independent economy, now became the focus of a small-holding peasant economy that apprentices hoped would guarantee their autonomy when full freedom came. Anderson's chronicle gives ample evidence of the praedials' strenuous efforts to secure the land and property they considered theirs, and to work there after meeting their forty-five hours per week obligation as apprentices. Legal title to this property, however, remained with the planters, whose attempts to thwart the apprentices' aspirations when freedom came, by making continued occupation of houses and grounds conditional on the workers' willingness to remain at work on the estate, would be contested for years after. Anderson, however, detected and documented the early manifestations of this conflict. He also chronicled the blossoming of social life among praedials as the apprentices exercised the new-found control over free time to indulge their interests in family, community, religion, recreation and leisure, assigning these pursuits priority over demands on their labour that they considered unjustified, or opportunities for work in a system they despised.

As is well-known, slaves were defined as chattels, as property. They were bought and sold as any other commodity; they were truly commodified. In the 1780s in St. Vincent, a healthy male slave was valued at about 50 pounds sterling. Spinelli calculates from the source material that the average value of a Vincentian slave, from 1822 to 1830, was 58 pounds, 6 shillings and 8 pence sterling. Prices were higher for male field slaves than for females or house servants.

Compensation to Slave-Owners

At Emancipation, the slave-owners were compensated for their slaves, who themselves received nothing compensatory for their years of slavery. The British government agreed to provide compensation for 22,997 slaves in St. Vincent who were valued by their owners at one million, three hundred and forty one thousand, four hundred and ninety-two pounds sterling or approximately 58 pounds sterling per slave. The Emancipation package to the slave-owners from the British was actually 592,509 pounds sterling, an average of 26 pounds sterling per slave or some 45 percent of their estimated worth, according to their owners. In today's value the compensation received would amount to approximately 118 million pounds sterling or 200 times the value of 1834. Clearly, an unanswerable case exists for Britain to pay St. Vincent and the Grenadines, and other Caribbean countries, appropriate and sufficient reparations as compensation for slavery. Reparations, too, are in order for the genocide committed against the thousands of the Kalinago and Garifuna people, the forced deportation of 5,080 of them to Rattan Island, off the coast of Honduras, and the confiscation of their lands. A vigorous and coordinated campaign is required globally for reparations.

The Causes of Slavery's End

It is now settled in modern Caribbean historiography that while abolitionists in Europe, such as William Wilberforce and others in Britain, contributed to the agitation which partly moved the British Parliament to pass the "Act for the Abolition of Slavery", it was, as reflected in the title of Richard Hart's celebrated book (two volumes), first published in 1985, the *Slaves Who Abolished Slavery*. The individual acts of defiance by slaves, including individual acts of violence, slave rebellions across the Caribbean, and the Haitian revolution led by slaves, precipitated slavery's end. The context for slavery's termination, as Eric Williams reminds us in his widely-acclaimed text, *Capitalism and Slavery*, revolved around the fact that slavery, which had facilitated the development of mercantile capitalism to industrial capitalism, had itself now become a brake on the further expansion of industrial capitalism in the early 19th century, and thus had to go.

Richard Hart instructs on this raft of issues:

> Revelling in Britain's liberal image earned by the abolition of the slave trade and slavery, most historians have paid little or no attention to the frequent and formidable rebellions and conspiracies of the slaves, or the extent to which these events influenced the British decision....The focal point around which the political history of the West Indies revolved for upwards of two centuries was the refusal of large numbers of the involuntary migrants from Africa passively to accept their enslavement. European opposition to slavery was aroused and grew over the years not only in response to the class interests of the rising bourgeoisie but also because the slaves in the sugar colonies were continually offering and conspiring to offer violent resistance. The idea, sedulously disseminated, that the enslavement of Africans was part of the natural order of things, was challenged again and again, as much by the casualties among the whites engaged in the trade and employed on the plantations as by the disclosure of the sufferings endured by the blacks.

All over St. Vincent, including the Grenadines, there were numerous individual and collective acts of resistance by slaves to their condition, which acts truly frightened the slave-owners and colonial authorities. Repression did not dull the slaves' resistance; and so-called amelioration only whetted their appetites for freedom.

Eric Williams' detailed documentation of the immense contribution to Britain's capitalist expansion by its slave-based colonies, and sugar plantations, in the West Indies, is available in his *Capitalism and Slavery* published in 1944. Long before that, however, Karl Marx in *Capital* (Volume 1, Chapter XXXI) published in 1867 had concluded:

> The discovery of gold and silver in America, the extirpation, enslavement and entombment in mines of the aboriginal population, the beginning of the conquest and looting of the East Indies, the turning of Africa into a warren for the commercial hunting of black-skins, signalised (sic) the rosy dawn of the era of capitalist production. These idyllic proceedings are the chief momenta of primitive accumulation.
>
> The colonial system ripened, like a hothouse, trade and navigation....The treasures captured outside Europe by undisguised looting, enslavement and murder, floated back to the mother country and were turned into capital.

It is this very capital which fuelled the development of industrial capitalism which the slave mode of production in the West Indies and its restrictive exchange relations externally, conspired to retard. The rising bourgeoisie in Europe had little patience with this retardation and were resolved to remove the barriers. The abolitionists' evangelising resonated with this rising and strong bourgeoisie not so much on a moral basis but on economic grounds.

Eric Williams succinctly addressed all this in *Capitalism and Slavery*:

> Whereas before, in the eighteenth century, every important vested interest in England was lined up on the side of monopoly and the colonial system; after 1783, one by one, every one of those interests came out against monopoly and the West Indian slave system. British exports to the world in manufactured goods which could be paid for only in raw materials — the cotton of the United States, the cotton, coffee and sugar of Brazil, the sugar of Cuba, the sugar and cotton of India. The expansion of British exports depended on the capacity of Britain to absorb the raw materials as payment. The British West Indian monopoly, prohibiting the importation of non-British plantation sugar for home consumption, stood in the way. Every imported vested interest — the cotton manufacturers, the ship owners, the sugar refiners; every important industrial and commercial town — London, Manchester, Liverpool, Birmingham, Sheffield, the West

Riding of Yorkshire, joined in the attack of West Indian slavery and West Indian monopoly. The abolitionists, significantly, concentrated their attack on the industrial centers.

More emphatically Williams wrote:

> The capitalists had first encouraged West Indian slavery and then helped to destroy it. When British capitalism depended on the West Indies, they ignored slavery or defended it. When British capitalism found the West Indian monopoly a nuisance, they destroyed the West Indian slavery as the first step in the destruction of West Indian monopoly. That slavery to them was relative and not absolute, and depended on latitude and longitude, it proved after 1833 by their attitude to slavery in Cuba, Brazil, and the United States. They taunted their opponents with seeing slavery only where they saw sugar and limiting their observation to the circumference of the hogshead. They refused to frame their tariff on grounds of morality, erect a pulpit in every custom house, and make their landing-waiters enforce anti-slavery doctrines.

C. L. R. James in *The Black Jacobins: Toussaint L'Ouverture and the San Domingo Revolution* published in 1963 was to make a similar bundle of arguments. Additionally he said something else of profundity and relevance:

> Great men make history, but only such history as it is possible for them to make. Their freedom of achievement is limited by the necessities of their environment. To portray the limits of those necessities and the realisation, complete or partial, of all possibilities, that is the true business of the historian.

In this he echoed Karl Marx in *The Eighteenth Brumaire of Louis Napoleon* published in 1869:

> Men make their own history, but they do not make it just as they please; they do not make it under circumstances chosen by themselves, but under circumstances directly encountered, given and transmitted from the past.

Genocide, Slavery and Under-Development

Substantially, the root of the under-development of St. Vincent and the Grenadines can be traced to the genocide committed against the Kalinago/Garifuna, the establishment of slavery and its post-emancipation debilitations, the colonial-imperial project of governance and the consequential warped shaping of our people's socio-political consciousness. To be sure, colonial over-rule facilitated the entry of St. Vincent and the Grenadines into the commerce, science and technology of a global industrial capitalism and its out-growths. It is true, too, that a bundle of liberal democratic institutions (the legislature, the executive, the judiciary, the public service, fundamental rights and the rule of law) were, over time, bequeathed to us. But the global embrace through commerce and technology and the liberal-democratic bequests were surely attainable, even if not necessarily at the same pace or in the same form, had our nation been allowed to remain on its own autochthonous or home-grown path under a self-governing entity from the very beginning. Comparative experiences indicate that this was most likely to have occurred without the debilitating hubris and incubus of the colonial-imperial project. This matter is far more fundamental than the simple drawing up of a check-list of "good" versus "bad" things about colonialism.

Let us look factually, for example, at the under-development of the areas of St. Vincent and the Grenadines occupied by the descendents of the Kalinago and Garifuna people. The British engaged in extraordinary acts of pillage and genocide against the indigenous population: Between 1763 and 1800, they were deprived of almost all of their 100,000 acres of land and pushed into a veritable reservation of inhospitable and largely unproductive lands of 238 aces in the north-east and adjoining north-west of St. Vincent. Further, several thousands of the young, productive men and women were killed by the British in the on-going genocidal wars against the Kalinago/Garifuna and 5,080 of them were forcibly deported to distant lands in Central America. These occurrences are a mere 215 or so years ago! Which people could have easily survived and thrived in the wake of such pillage, genocide, and forced deportations? Is there any wonder that they are among the poorest today in St. Vincent and the Grenadines despite enormous efforts by successive national administrations since the 1950s (government led by Ebenezer Joshua, Milton Cato, James Mitchell and Ralph Gonsalves) to improve their lot?

Similarly, some fifty years of the barbarism of slavery and monumental post-Emancipation neglect and oppression/exploitation of the former slaves and their descendants by British colonialism, had left the majority of the population of St. Vincent and the Grenadines in a cruel and harsh condition of under-development and poverty. Modern democratic governments and the post-1950s Vincentian society are still trying to come to grips with the burdens of underdevelopment, without compensating benefits, handed to us by the colonial-imperial project. Thus, the on-going quest for better lives, productive endeavours, a good society, and the further ennoblement of the Vincentian component of our Caribbean civilisation.

Indeed, as Walter Rodney has instructed us in *How Europe Underdeveloped Africa*, published in 1972, under-development inevitably occurs in a nation which becomes subordinated to an external colonial or imperial power. Rodney advises as follows:

> When two societies of different sorts come into prolonged and effective contact, the rate and character of change taking place in both is seriously affected to the extent that entirely new patterns are created. Two general rules can be observed to apply in such cases. First, the weaker of the two societies (i.e. the one with less economic capacity) is bound to be adversely affected --- and the bigger the gap between the two societies concerned the more detrimental are the consequences. For example, when European capitalism came into contact with the indigenous hunting societies of America and the Caribbean, the latter were virtually exterminated. Second, assuming the weaker society does survive, then ultimately it can resume its own independent development only if it proceeds to a higher level than that of the economy which had previously dominated it.

In addressing the specific issue of "underdevelopment", Rodney identifies two ideas of relevance: the first is that it is a comparative concept; and the second, a dialectical relationship. He addresses this second issue, thus:

> A second and even more indispensable component of modern underdevelopment is that it expresses a particular relationship of exploitation: namely, the exploitation of one country by another.

All the countries named as 'underdeveloped' in the world are exploited by others; and the underdevelopment with which the world is now preoccupied is a product of capitalist, imperialist, and colonialist exploitation. African and Asian societies were developing independently until they were taken over directly or indirectly by capitalist powers. When that happened, exploitation increased and the export of surplus ensued, depriving the societies of the benefit of their natural resources and labour. That is an integral part of underdevelopment in the contemporary sense.

Rodney's conclusion is telling in addressing the condition of Africa, and I consider it apt in relation to St. Vincent and the Grenadines:

The only positive development in colonialism was when it ended.... In contrast to a subjective interpretation of what was good about colonialism on the one hand and what was bad on the other hand, there is the approach which follows closely the aims and achievements of the colonizers and the counter claims and achievements of the African people. Sometimes Africans were restricted merely to manipulating colonial institutions as best they could; but, in addition, certain fundamental contradictions arose within colonial society, and they could only be resolved by Africans' regaining their sovereignty as a people.

The colonial apologist, and even racist, John Anderson tells us something quite interesting in his *Journal* written in 1836 of the defeated Kalinago/Garifuna nation:

It is certainly a surprising fact, that so insignificant a body as the Caribs amounted to when finally transported to the island of Rattan in the bay of Honduras, (being in all 5,080 men, women, and children) in March 1797, should for 2 years have baffled the energies of Great Britain! It speaks little for the military skill of the Generals employed, even allowing that the localities of the isle are favourable to a Guerilla warfare. With their extinction as a warlike nation...every energy seems to have expired: The few Caribs who are allowed to exist in the Northern quarter, (which is designated by their name), are a wretched remnant...weak in body as in mind; with an innate abhorrence of labour...looking upon idleness as the 'summum bonum' (highest good) of life. They are still divided into yellow, and Black Caribs...the latter sprung from the aborigines, and Negro slaves.... Being passionately fond of spirits, the planters occasionally succeed in rousing them (the Caribs) from their torpid state by the temptation of rum, when they will assist in shipping off the sugars from estates. In every other respect they are useless to themselves or others.

Please note that genocide, forced deportations, land deprivations, defeat and death of their leader, Chief Chatoyer, had made a proud, independent, tenacious people *"a wretched remnant – weak in body as in mind."* That is what a pillaging and rapacious British colonialism did to the Kalinago/Garifuna nation! Similarly, slavery had dehumanised productive, self-governing Africans, brutalised them on the plantations, robbed them of their dignity and the value of their labour, and denied them opportunities for socio-economic advancement and equality in the decades after Emancipation. All that and more, constitutes the root of underdevelopment.

Emancipation to Independence

There are those who incorrectly assert, with only a nodding, stylised acquaintance with the facts of our journey from emancipation to independence (1834 to 1979 and thereafter), that "slavery" still exists in St. Vincent and the Grenadines or that nothing has really changed since the end of slavery for the bulk of labouring people. Clearly, that position is wholly unsustainable when one examines every single index of progress or development whether lodged in the material, social, cultural, legal, political, and ideational spheres of life.

Still, though, the process of our people's emancipation is yet to be completed: Significant poverty levels still exist; underdevelopment still persists though in altered and less harsh dimensions; the colonial-imperial ideological or ideational hubris still retards a developed, national and people-centered consciousness; the development of our political economy is yet to escape the debilitating embrace of an economic and political imperialism; our cultural parameters are defined substantially by the cultural behemoth of a global empire, despite genuine resistance from several quarters; and the quest for independent political and economic spaces is encumbered by backward forces within our nation, inclusive of the diaspora, and exploitative forces outside our national boundaries.

Successive waves of the socio-democratic struggles of our people since emancipation have sought to advance popular liberation and development in all spheres. The efforts of my government are part and parcel of these ongoing social-democratic struggles and quests.

I affirm unequivocally that the Unity Labour Party (ULP) administrations from 2001 to 2012, and continuing, despite their weaknesses and limitations, have articulated a compelling narrative for home-grown development, in concerted solidarity with nations and peoples overseas, have fashioned appropriate mechanisms to implement this "compelling narrative", and have achieved commendable successes in this regard. Our solid record for further liberation and development in every single area of public policy and human endeavours stands objective scrutiny. But the journey is still incomplete; important tasks are yet to be finished and some have barely started; there are still many burdens and crosses to bear; and many more rivers to cross. But our nation is up to it all; and we in the ULP are fairly well-placed and fairly well-equipped, better by far than any other political party, in communion with the people and other non-state actors, to continue to lead the charge for further progress.

I remind everyone that the ULP's "compelling narrative" consists of a people-centred vision; a social-democratic philosophy adapted to the practical conditions of St. Vincent and the Grenadines and our Caribbean; a comprehensive economic strategy and accompanying bundle of tactics in a quest to construct a modern, competitive, post-colonial economy which is at once national, regional, and global; a socio-cultural rubric for the further ennoblement of our Caribbean civilization and its magnificent Vincentian component; a creative menu of practical policies and detailed programmes touching and concerning every area of public policy and relevant human activities, including the economy, the physical infrastructure and housing, health and education, social security and social development, sports and culture, good governance and citizen security, regional integration and foreign policy.

On this the 178th anniversary since the passage of the "Act for the Abolition of Slavery in Saint Vincent and its Dependencies" in 1834, all of us must redouble our efforts for further individual and collective liberation and development. Each of us must work most productively and in solidarity with others; each of us must exhibit the virtue of "good neighborliness"; we must seek to raise our national and social consciousness and emancipate ourselves from "mental slavery"; we must own our institutions and our government; we must constitute ourselves as an active, participatory citizenry; we must act out our belief in our self-mastery, confident that no one is better than us even while we acknowledge humbly that we are not better than anyone else, only different; and we must make every effort to control our destinies, in solidarity with our friends and allies. Above all we must know ourselves, our possibilities and limitations. We must be determined to strengthen our possibilities and lessen our limitations as far as is humanly possible. We must turn setbacks into advances, consolidate our advances and make them permanent. In the process, we reaffirm that we are a nation founded upon the belief in the supremacy of God and the freedom and dignity of man!

Let this period in commemoration of Emancipation Day, August 01, 2012, be a time for reflection, love and caring, and commitment to do good today, much better than yesterday and even better yet tomorrow. We come from yesterday with our burdens and weaknesses; we go forward tomorrow with our strengths and possibilities.

This is an apt occasion for all of us who now constitute an integrated creolised whole known as the Vincentian component of our Caribbean civilisation everyone whatever his or her ethnic or social background to let the poetic words of the iconic Guyanese Martin Carter ring out from the last stanza of his celebrated "I Come From the Nigger Yard":

> I come from the nigger yard of yesterday
> leaping from the oppressor's hate
> and the scorn of myself.
> I come to the world with scars upon my soul
> wounds on my body, fury in my hands.
> I turn to the histories of men and the lives of the peoples.
> I examine the shower of the sparks the wealth of the dreams.

I am pleased with the glories and sad with the sorrows
rich with the riches, poor with the loss.
From the nigger yard of yesterday I come with my burden.
To the world of tomorrow I turn with my strength.

II.
Preliminary Notes on the Quantification of Reparation from the British for Lands Stolen, for Genocide and Forcible Deportation of the Garifuna People, and for Enslavement of Africans in St. Vincent and the Grenadines

The Issue

The case for reparations from the British for lands "stolen", for genocide and forced deportation of the Garifuna people, and for the enslavement of Africans in St. Vincent and the Grenadines is unanswerably strong. This case has been made repeatedly, and cogently, elsewhere by a number of persons, including me. The latest Caribbean scholar to do so is Professor Hilary Mc. D. Beckles in his recent book *Britain's Black Debt: Reparations for Caribbean Slavery and Native Genocide* (University of the West Indies Press, Mona, Jamaica, 2013). Professor Beckles did not expressly include lands "stolen" in his analysis, but I do so here. I put "stolen" in inverted commas because, land cannot be stolen according to English law in that it cannot be moved or transported. I use the expression "stolen" in this context to mean that the British forcibly deprived the Garifuna (Black Caribs) and the Kalinago (Yellow Caribs) people of their land and *profited* directly from such forcible and illegal, appropriation of land.

It is to be noted that the British were not invited to St. Vincent and the Grenadines by the Garifuna and the Kalinago. The British acquired suzerainty over St. Vincent and the Grenadines in 1763 after the end of the Seven Years' War with France, at the Treaty of Paris. There was in that Treaty a general carve up of other people's lands, including St. Vincent and the Grenadines, by the colonial powers of Britain and France.

A Note on the Size of St. Vincent and the Grenadines

St. Vincent and the Grenadines admeasures 150 square miles or 96,000 acres of land. The main island St. Vincent admeasures 133 square miles or 85,120 acres. The Grenadine islands admeasure 17 square miles or 10,880 acres. Roughly two-thirds of St. Vincent and the Grenadines, at all material times, has been available for agriculture, public works, houses, and buildings for businesses and other public use. Thus, 32,000 acres have been in forests or other reserves; and 64,000 acres have existed below the 1,000 feet contour for cultivation and physical development.

Garifuna/Kalinago Land 1763-1800

General Overview

One of the first acts of the British colonizers in 1764 was to declare that all land in St. Vincent and the Grenadines (the country was called St. Vincent prior to independence in 1979) belonged to the British Crown. At one stroke they deprived the Garifuna and the Kalinago people of all their land which was held in common by them, save and except for under 2,000 acres which they allowed French settlers to occupy and cultivate on the western side of St. Vincent. The British government permitted the French to remain on these lands but only as leasehold tenants for up to a maximum of forty years.

The British over-rule of St. Vincent was unbroken from 1763 until internal self-government in 1969 and formal independence in 1979 save and except for a brief period, 1779 to 1783, when the French temporarily dislodged British occupation and settlement.

From 1764 until 1795, the Garifuna/Kalinago nation fought the British Colonisers. The land issue was central to the popular native resistance to British colonisation. Bit-by-bit, chunk-by-chunk, the British took the lands of the Garifuna on one pretext after another. The British finally defeated the Garifuna/Kalinago people in 1795 and in subsequent skirmishes. On March 14, 1795, a British ambush and massacre of the Garifuna patriots occasioned the death of the Paramount Chief Joseph Chatoyer, leader of the Garifuna people. (The Right Excellent Joseph Chatoyer was formally declared as the First National Hero of St. Vincent and the Grenadines on March 14, 2002).

By 1800, the Garifuna/Kalinago people were practically quarantined on an allocated parcel of 238 acres of land in an inaccessible area of the north east of St. Vincent. Thus, between 1763 and 1800, a mere 37 years, the Garifuna/Kalinago people lost the remainder of their 85,120 acres of land on St. Vincent and the 10,880 acres in the Grenadines. The British government must pay for these lands from which the British Treasury and its grantees benefited directly to the detriment of the Garifuna/Kalinago nation and their successors in independent St. Vincent and the Grenadines.

Some Relevant Details of the British Land and Sales and Grants

In 1764, the British government granted to General Robert Monckton, a "hero" of the Seven Years' War, 4,000 acres of land on the Windward coast of St. Vincent. Monckton was the General who had captured St. Vincent and Martinique in the war against the French. The 4,000 acres of land given to Monckton was between what is today Biabou Village on the north and Stubbs Village on the south, extending inland to the headwaters of the rivers flowing from the Mesopotamia Valley. It is on over 400 acres of these lands that the Argyle International Airport is being currently built.

Monckton never settled his land but sold it instead for £30,000 (thirty thousand pounds sterling) at an average of £7.10 shillings per acre.

In today's value £30,000 pounds amounts to £27.0 million, using a factor of 900 (based on wage values; a factor of 829 has been used by Professor Draper of the University College of London to equate 1833 values with today's). Thus, it amounts to EC $112.9 million in today's value. [£1.0 = EC $4.18 on April 05, 2013]. This incidentally amounts to EC $28,215 per acre in today's terms, which is in fact much below the current price for these lands.

Note: There will be debate on the size of the factor to be used in assessing comparative values but that used herein is soundly-based.

In 1764, the British government auctioned 20,538 acres on St. Vincent. On this sale, the British Treasury earned £162,854 (One hundred and sixty-two thousand, eight hundred and fifty-four pounds sterling), an average of £7.16 shillings per acre.

In today's value the calculation is as follows:

£162,854 x by a factor of 900 = £146.59 million or EC $612.7 million.

Between 1776 and 1779, a further 2,156 acres of land were disposed of by the British government through Governor Valentine Morris. This disposition of land ignored the boundaries of the 1773 "settlement" with the Caribs/Garifuna. Sixty-four grants were made to 56 persons, 18 of these were to French settlers. Of these new grants, 37 were under 50 acres in size. Only Governor Morris' grants to himself were larger than 100 acres in size. In fact, Morris reserved for himself 3 large parcels of 350, 360, and 500 acres, located in the newly-opened Carib lands north of the Yambou River. At an estimated £7.10 shillings per acre, the British Treasury collected £16,170.

In today's value the calculation is as follows:

£16,170 x by a factor of 900 = £14.55 million or EC $60.8 million.

Appendices 1 and 2 provide interesting summarises touching and concerning land in 1777.

A large tract of land was granted by the Colonial Governor Morris in St. Vincent to Lt. Colonel George Etherington on the northwest Leeward Coast. The actual size of the grant is unknown but it was north of, and bounded on the south by, the Wallilabou River. Interestingly, it was while using garrison troops to clear his land that Etherington allowed a French force to capture St. Vincent in 1779 without firing a shot.

Note: Between 1779 and 1784, St. Vincent was under French rulership. During this time, a "Dame d'honneur" in the French Palace, Martha Swinburne, was granted 20,000 acres of unoccupied land. The exact location is unknown. These lands reverted to the British after they re-conquered and re-occupied St. Vincent.

In 1802, the new British Governor of St. Vincent Henry Bentinck (who succeeded his father, William Bentinck) conveyed the right "to use" but not "to own" 5,262 acres of land on the Windward coast, which formed part of "Carib Country", to war veterans.

Then in 1807, a domestic crisis erupted for the British Governor when the occupiers of these lands discovered that an American Royalist from Georgia (USA), Colonel Thomas Brown, had been granted 6,000 acres of "Carib Country" lands, stretching from the Byera River in the south to Cayo River in the north. This grant included the lands of the occupiers.

Negotiations ensued to resolve this "land crisis". The upshot was that Colonel Brown was allowed to keep 1,600 acres plus an indemnity of £25,000, part of the Treasury's earnings from the eventual sale of the occupied lands (4,400 acres) to their occupiers at an average price per acre of £22.10 shillings. These lands included some of the best sugar cane land on St. Vincent. They included the following seven (7) estates: Tourama, Orange Hill, Waterloo, Lot No. 14, Rabacca, Langley Park, and Mt. Bentinck. Colonel Brown's estate of 1,600 acres was Grand Sable Estate.

The 4,400 sold to the "occupiers" earned the Treasury £99,000 (4,400 acres x £22.5 per acre).

Using a factor of 850 to arrive at today's value of the 1807 values, the value today is calculated thus: £99,000 x 850 = £84.15 million or EC $351.7 million.

Colonel Brown's estate of 1,600 acres was valued at £36,000 (1,600 x £22.5 per acre).

The calculation for today's value is thus:

£36,000 x 850 = £30.6 million or EC $127.9 million.

In all, therefore, today's value of these 6,000 acres in the aggregate amounts to £114.75 or EC $479.7 million.

It is to be noted, in summary, that the actual values for lands sold, in today's value, for which evidence is provided here are as follows:

(i)	Monckton's 4,000 acres	:	EC$112.9 m
(ii)	British government's saleof 20,538 acres	:	EC$612.7 m
(iii)	Sale of 2,156 acres between 1776 and 1779	:	EC$ 60.8 m
(iv)	Colonel Brown's 6,000 acres	:	EC$479.7 m
	Thus for 32,694 acres	:	EC$1,266 bn

Please note that these lands were sold between 1764 and 1807. Later sales would have been at higher values. (The data above are available, in the main, from Joseph Spinelli's doctoral dissertation entitled *Land Use and Population in St. Vincent, 1763–1960*, University of Florida, 1973.)

Note: By 1819, it was assessed that the land on the main island, St. Vincent, below the 1,000 feet contour which was available for cultivation amounted to 48,474 acres. Obviously, not all these cultivable lands were of the same value. By 1827, there were 110 privately-owned estates in St. Vincent and the Grenadines. On St. Vincent there were 97 estates covering an aggregate of 35,755 acres; on Bequia there were nine (9) estates with an aggregate of 3,698 acres; on Mustique, two (2) estates of 2,675 acres in all; on Canouan, one estate of 600 acres; and in Union Island, one estate of 2,057 acres. The details are in Appendix 3.

Conclusion

The commercially usable land of all of St. Vincent (including the Grenadines), that is to say land which was below the 1,000 feet contour and not provided for as "forest reserve", was roughly two-thirds of the 96,000 acreage or 64,000 acres in the year 1800. "Commercially usable" includes agriculture, public works, houses, businesses.

On the basis of the values which were established in fact, let us be conservative and assess one-half of the 64,000 acres at £11.25 per acre and the other one-half at £22.5 per acre.

Thus, the colonial government had a total value as follows:

(a)	32,000 at £11.25 per acre	:	£ 360,000;	
(b)	32,000 at £22.5 per acre	:	£ 720,000	
		Total :	£1,080,000	

Today's value is thus calculated: £1.08 million x by a factor of 850 = £918 million or EC $3.84 billion. In today's terms this amounts to roughly EC $1.40 per square foot!

Reparations for Genocide

Estimates of the Garifuna and Kalinago population vary. Valentine Morris, the British Governor of St. Vincent, asserted in 1774 that there "cannot be less than five thousand five hundred or even approaching six thousand" of the Caribs (Garifuna and Kalinago). This number he said was "exclusive of runaway negroes".

In 1777 Governor Morris was of the view that (of) "the original possessors of the Island or real Charibs...scarce forty of these now remain alive."

In 1795, N. Dickinson puts the Black Carib population between eight-to-nine thousand. In 1795, too, Alexander Anderson estimates the Black Carib population at nine thousand (see Appendix 4 of *The Black Carib Wars: Freedom, Survival and the Making of the Garifuna* authored by Christopher Taylor and published by Signal Books Limited of Oxford, United Kingdom, in 2012).

So, let us take the Garifuna and Kalinago population in St. Vincent in 1795 at nine thousand.

Between July 26th 1796 and February 2nd 1797, 4,776 persons from St. Vincent were sent to the inhospitable off-shore island of Balliceaux for a seven-month transit before deportation to the Spanish-ruled Roatan Island in the bay of Honduras in Central America. Of this 4,776, the overwhelming number were Garifuna (4,633), and 102 Kalinagos (Yellow Caribs) and 41 African slaves. There were 1,080 men; 2,003 women; and 1,693 children. (Eighty-three of "the Yellow Caribs" were sent back to St. Vincent; 22 died on Balliceaux).

So, of the 4,693 (4776 minus the 83 Kalinagos) on Balliceaux, only 2,248 embarked on the journey to Roatan Island on March 09, 1797. This meant that 2,445 died on Balliceaux. The journey to Roatan reduced their number further by 222. So, on April 12, 1797, a total of 2,026 Garifuna landed at Roatan: 664 were men, 1,362 were women and children.

By March 1797, it has been estimated that less than 2,000 Garifuna survived to remain in St. Vincent. Remember that in 1795, there were 9,000 Garifuna. Four thousand six hundred and sixty three (4,693) were dragooned to Balliceaux. It means therefore that some 2,500 Garifuna were killed in battle or massacred in the aftermath of Chatoyer's death and the suppression of the Garifuna guerilla resistance to the British. This number (2,500) plus those who died from maltreatment and disease on Balliceaux (2,445) and those who died en route to forcible exile in Roatan (222) amount to an aggregate of 5,167 or some 57 percent of the Garifuna nation in St. Vincent in 1797.

This is an incredible, historic crime of genocide for which the British must pay appropriate recompense to the nation of St. Vincent and the Grenadines, including the descendants of the Garifuna. Appropriate recompense is required, too, for those communities of Garifuna in Belize, Nicaragua, Honduras, and Guatemala who remain disadvantaged up to today. It is to be noted that the British exterminated from St. Vincent through genocide (5,167) and forced deportation (2,026) some 7,193 Garifuna people or roughly 80 percent of the Garifuna nation on St. Vincent. This is a horrendous statistic for which the British nation is culpable and responsible.

So, for reparation purposes, what value do we put on the lives of our Garifuna brothers and sisters who were victims of genocide and forced deportation? We need to look comparatively at the compensation package offered, for example, to the Jews who suffered at the hands of Adolph Hitler's Nazis. We need to fine-tune our work in this regard. Clearly, billions of dollars are in order for recompense for genocide and forcible deportation of the Garifuna people and the ruination of their nation. This is a big number yet to be quantified.

Reparations for Slavery in St. Vincent and the Grenadines

There are at least three categories of reparations for slavery: First, the precise recompense which was paid to the proprietors of slaves by the British Government consequent upon the passage of the Abolition of Slavery Act in 1833. Secondly, the additional value of the slaves which ought to have been paid and was not paid; that is to say the actual valuation of the slaves as generally agreed at the time. And thirdly, general damages or compensation for slavery, including exemplary and aggravated damages.

First, the British government paid the owners of the slaves in St. Vincent the aggregate sum of £592,509 for 22,997 slaves (as per the last registration in 1832) at an average of £26 per slave or £21,554 (EC $90,095.00) in today's values. The actual compensation was as follows:

Field slaves", who made up 69 percent of the total slave population, were compensated at £31 per slave;

"Non-field slaves", who accounted for 13 percent of the slave population, were compensated at £30 per slave;

"Children under 6 years" comprised 13 percent of the slave population and were valued at £11 each; and

"Aged and Infirm" amounted to 5 percent of the total slave population and were valued at £3 each.

Professor Draper and his team at the University College of London who have been working on this issue of "the compensated value" of slaves, consider authoritatively that a factor of 829 be used to calculate the present day monetary value of the compensation paid in 1833 – 1834 to the slave-owners.

Thus, in St. Vincent, £592,509 multiplied by a factor of 829 gives an aggregate present-day value of £491.18 million or EC $2.05 billion.

Second, the slave-owners in St. Vincent insisted that the compensation paid to them was some 45 percent of the market value of their slaves at the time. Most experts agree that this was so.

Thus, if the full market value is to be paid to the descendants of these slaves through the nation of St. Vincent and the Grenadines (the overwhelming majority of whose nationals are the descendants of the slaves), the full 1833 value of £1,341,492 or approximately £58 per slave, converted into today's value would be £1.11 billion or EC $4.6 billion. The compensation formula thus is: £1,341,492 x 829 = £1.11 billion or EC $4.6 billion.

Third, the question of general damages, exemplary and aggravated damages as compensation generally for slavery, pain, suffering, and genocide has to be assessed technically. This, too, is a huge number. Historians, economists, and legal experts have to work together to arrive at an appropriate number.

It is important to note that incomplete records show that 62,176 enslaved Africans left for St. Vincent in the period 1764 to 1807. Of this number, 55,562 on 240 voyages arrived in St. Vincent. Please note the extent of the high attrition rate of the slave population even after births to the enslaved Africans are taken into account. It should be pointed out that 61.8 percent of the landed slaves were males; 23.3 percent, females; and 14.9 percent, children. Towards slavery's end in 1832, there were

22,997 registered slaves. (The Slave Trade Database compiled by Emory University et al is in the source for embarkations and disembarkations of slaves. See Appendix 4.)

Partial Summation

Reparations for Garifuna land in St. Vincent and the Grenadines: EC $3.84 billion.

Reparations for Genocide of at least 5,167 of the Garifuna People (57 percent of the Garifuna nation): Quantification to be determined after further study.

Reparations for forced deportation and exile of 2,026 Garifuna: Quantification to be determined after further study.

Reparations for slavery in St. Vincent and the Grenadines:_Actual compensation paid to slave-owners by British government in today's value: EC $2.05 billion; or preferably the actual market value of the 22,997 slaves in today's value: EC $4.6 billion.

General damages, exemplary and aggravated damages for compensation for slavery in St. Vincent and the Grenadines: Quantification to be determined after further study.

How to Proceed with Quantification Issue?

I have attempted a rough quantification of the damage and loss to the people of St. Vincent and the Grenadines as a consequence of "theft" of lands, native genocide and slavery in St. Vincent and the Grenadines by the colonial power of Britain. This exercise has been done through a joinder of the factual historical matrices and the application of normal legal principles of an ordinary claim in civil suit in a domestic jurisdiction. I have done so to indicate the enormity of the sums involved.

Clearly, this is not an "ordinary case" for a domestic jurisdiction in view of the attendant juridical/legal hurdles which one would have to confront.

Thus, an option would be to proceed in an appropriate international legal forum, grounded upon breaches of international treaties which possibly raise recompense or reparations on the basis of the legacy of under-development occasioned by the colonial plunder of lands, native genocide, and slavery.

But this quest for recompense or reparations must be connection, in some meaningful way, to the indicational quantification outlined above. In short, the reparations sought must be substantial. It ought to be more than an apology, reconciliation, and "legacy" contributions, vital as they are.

These are on-going considerations for the reparations movement to reflect further upon.

A Note on Further Action

Reparations Committees for Slavery have been established in Jamaica, Barbados, and Antigua-Barbuda. The Cabinet of St. Vincent and the Grenadines has decided, in principle, to establish a Reparations Committee on "Stolen Lands", Genocide and Forcible Deportation of the Garifuna, and for Slavery. Its membership is to be named shortly.

We must push for a CARICOM Commission on Reparations. This is urgent.

We must continue to advocate for reparations in all international fora.

We must continue to educate our Caribbean people and our diaspora, and lift their awareness of the reparations issue.

We must assemble a competent body of experts to prepare the case, including the sums required as reparations.

We must establish links with other populations who seek or have sought reparations, including the descendants of African slaves internationally, indigenous populations globally, Jews and Palestinians.

A regional conference on reparations must be held urgently. St. Vincent and the Grenadines is prepared to host it.

A Final Note on Reparations for Haiti

In a book *An Unbroken Agony: Haiti, From Revolution to the Kidnapping of a President* (Basic Civitas Books, 2007), its author, the well-known American fighter for justice internationally, Randall Robinson, provides a gripping account of France's successful demand for reparations from Haiti for loss of property (including slaves) at the time of the Haitian Revolution. This payment of reparations from Haiti to France has contributed immensely to Haiti's underdevelopment. It is a tale of imperialism's unjust power and might over a poor, relatively defenseless nation.

The basic facts are these:

By 1825, twenty-two years after the death of Toussaint L'Ouverture, the Haitian army was a weakened and divided force. France threatened to re-enslave Haitians, and imposed an ordinance requiring from Haiti a payment of 150 million francs and a 50 percent tariff reduction for all French ships docking in Haiti. To meet the first payment of 30 million francs under the ordinance, the government of Haiti had to borrow the full amount from a private French bank, MM Ch Ternaux Grandolphe et Cie.

In 1838, after extensive negotiations, under a French-Haitian Traité d'Armité (Treaty of Friendship), the original obligation of 150 million francs was reduced to 90 million francs; thus, a balance of 60 million francs was to be paid. Haiti was required to make annual payments of 2 million francs over 30 years. These payments were in addition to repayment on the original 30 million francs from the first private bank. Haiti was thus coerced into borrowing commercially to pay a hugely unjust obligation to France.

As late as 1915, or 111 years after the successful slave revolution in Haiti, some 80 percent of the Haitian government's budget was being paid out in debt service to French and American banks on loans that had been contracted for Haiti to pay reparations to France.

In 1922, seven years into a 19-year American military occupation of Haiti that resulted in the death of 15,000 Haitians, the USA imposed a US $16 million loan to the Haitian government to pay off its "debt" to France.

The American loan was finally paid off in 1947. Haiti was left virtually bankrupt and impoverished. It has never recovered.

In the early years of the 21st century, President Jean Bertrand Aristide of Haiti pushed the issue of righting this historic wrong. He made the demand for reparations from France for slavery and genocide.

Aristide was involuntarily removed from office. Did his call for reparations lead to his fall from office? Many thoughtful people think so, although the matter is complicated.

A CARICOM push for reparations must include Haiti.

Appendix 1

General State and Disposition of Lands in St. Vincent, as Described by Mr. Byers, in His Survey Made January, 1777

		Acres
1.	Lands sold at Public Sale by the Commissioners, leased, and appropriated for public uses	20,392
2.	Lands "granted" by British to friendly Caribs	1,210
3.	Lands "granted" to Lt. General Monckton	4,000
4.	Lands "Granted" to the Caribs by Treaty in 1773	27,628
5.	Cultivated lands undisposed of	9,777
6.	"Impracticable" (uncultivatable) Land	21,079
	Total	84,286
	Note: The Carib lands in 4 above were by 1805 all seized by the British; by 1805 the Caribs (Garifuna) were legally prohibited from owning lands.	

Appendix 2

Estate Lands in St. Vincent in 1777

PARISH	ACRES
Charlotte Parish	11,849
St. George's Parish	9,337
St. Andrew's Parish	4,096
St. David's Parish	4,198
St. Patrick's Parish	5,426
Total	34,906

Appendix 3

Estate Holdings in St. Vincent and the Grenadines in the Year 1827

(A)	CHARLOTTE PARISH		
	Name/Location of Estate	Owners	Acres
1.	Adelphi	Devisees of Charles Jnr; ½; John Birch and Ann Montgomery, his wife, ¼; Sarah Grant, 1/8; and Geo. Colquhoun Grant, 1/8.	666
2.	New Adelphi	Warner Ottley	642
3.	Belle Vue	Devisees of John Gerard	440
4.	Colonarie Vale	Walter Coningham	407
5.	Cummacrabou	Ellen and Maria Cruickshank	200
6.	Dumbarton	W. M'Gowne and the Heirs of John Johnson	224
7.	Grand Sable	Devisees of Thomas Browne, Deceased	1,600
8.	Jambou Vale	Devisees of E. Fleming Akers	300
9.	Langley Park	John Cruickshank	600
10.	Lot, No. 14	Alexander Cumming	600
11.	Mt. Bentinck	Devisees of John and Robert Dalzell	750
12.	Mt. Grennan	Devisees of Robert Glasgow, deceased	367
13.	Mt. William	Heirs of Valentine and Malachi O'Connor	460
14.	New Prospect	James Symon	240
15.	Orange Hill	James Sutherland, Geo. Mackay Sutherland, Ewen Baillie Sutherland, ½; the devisees of Thomas Paterson, ½	400
16.	Park Hill	Allan Macdowall	350

17.	Peruvian Vale	Devisees of George Whitfield, deceased	633
18.	Rabacca	Alexander Cumming	410
19.	Richland Park	Messrs. Penny and Ames	350
20.	Sans Souci	Devisees of Rob Glasgow, ½; and Alex Mc Barnet, ½.	297
21.	Spring	Rich. Nichol, ½; and the Devisees of John Nichol, deceased, ½	300
22.	Three Rivers	Harry Hackshaw	700
23.	Turama	Sir Alexander Mc Kenzie	600
24.	Union	John Roche Dusent	818
25.	Waterloo	James Sutherland, Geo. Mackay Sutherland, Ewen Baille Sutherland	410
26.	Fancy	Sir William John Struth	156
		(A) Sub-Total	12,920

(B) ST. GEORGE'S PARISH

27.	Aker's Marriaqua	Devisees of Edward Fleming Akers	119
28.	Argyle	Prince Polignac, ½; Archibald Mc Donald, ½	365
29.	Arnos Vale	Samuel Greathead	449
30.	Bellair	Francis Brown Douglas	401
31.	Belmont	John Pemberton Ross	256
32.	Belvidere	Thomas Hagart and Elizabeth, his wife	269
33.	Brighton	Gilbert Munro	400
34.	Calder	Prince Polignac and Archibald Mc Donald	350
35.	Calder Ridge	Prince Polignac and Archibald Mac Donald	194
36.	Cane Garden	Samuel Gregg	82
37.	Cane Hall	William Winn	392
38.	Carapan	Archibald and William Alves	240
39.	Coubamarou	Devisees of John Dalzell, deceased	181

40.	Diamond, Lower	Johnathan Morgan	199
41.	Diamond, Upper	Lady Bolton	189
42.	Escape	Johnathan Morgan	193
43.	Evesham Vale	James Huggins Lacroix	202
44.	Fairhall	James Adam Gordon	420
45.	Fountain	Rene Augier, Henry Lindow Lindow	300
46.	Golden Vale	James Lacroix	260
47.	Harmony Hall	Thomas Choppin	147
48.	Kingstown Park	Rev. Charles Paul	142
49.	Strowan Cottage	Richard Robertson	270
50.	Liberty Lodge	John Small	200
51.	Mt. Pleasant	Mrs. Douglas	306
52.	Prospect	Sir William John Struth	464
53.	Ratho Mill	Richard Rees	342
54.	Redemption	George Sharpe	600
55.	Revolution Hall	Wn. Glenn Ponsoby, John Ponsoby, George Ponsoby, and Taylor Hammond Ponsoby	186
56.	Richmond Hill	Charles James French	280
57.	Rivulet	Duncan Brown and Duncan Forbes Sutherland	230
58.	Sion Hill	Hon. W. Fraser, W.M. Alexander, Claude Neilson and Boyd Alexander	340
59.	Villa	Devisees of John Robley and Charles Brooke	339
		(B) Sub-Total	9,307

(C) ST. ANDREW'S PARISH

60.	Camden Park	Charles Phillips	330
61.	Cane Grove	James Wilson	598
62.	Cane Wood	Devisees of John Dalzell, deceased	541
63.	Clare Valley	John Snell	443
64.	Hope	John Inglet Fortescue	216
65.	L'Anse Joyeuse	Devisees of John B. Questel	190
66.	Montrose	Devisees of Andrew Rose	430

67.	Ottley Hall	William Boyd	200
68.	Pembroke	Devisees of John Robley and Charles Brooke	453
69.	Pennistons	Johnathan Morgan and _____ Jennings	250
70.	Queensbury	Leonard Slater	415
71.	Retreat	Devisees of Edward Jackson, deceased and Charles Kirby	n/a
		(C) Sub-Total	4,066

(D) ST. PATRICK'S PARISH

72.	Aker's Layou	Edmund Fleming Akers	250
73.	Belle Isle	John Greatheed	486
74.	Cumberland	Richard Rees	245
75.	Grove	Trustees of Mrs. Hill	315
76.	Kearton's	Mary Kearton and Henry Lindow Lindow	384
77.	L'Ance Mahaut	Thomas Wilkinson	176
78.	Mount Hope	Macduff Fyffe	173
79.	Mt. Wynne	Richard Nichol and Devisees of John Nichol	500
80.	Palmisle Park	Devisees of Edward Jackson	200
81.	Peter's Hope	Devisees of William Gurley	400
82.	Reversion	Devisees of Thomas Morgan, deceased	250
83.	Rutland Vale	Devisees of Josias Jackson	600
84.	Spring	Gordon Augustus Thomson	684
85.	Wallilabou	Alexander M'Barnet	500
86.	Westwood	Dr. Coull	265
		(D) Sub-Total	5,428

(E) ST. DAVID'S PARISH

87.	Belmont	Alexander Cruickshank	240

88.	Bostock Park	John and Nathaniel Bassutt Cropper and John Bolton	900
89.	Heirs of T. Fraser	Thomas Fraser	214
90.	Golden Grove	Christopher Punnett	350
91.	Millingtons	Thomas Crookenden	108
92.	Mt. Alexander	Devisees of J.D. Questel	300
93.	Petit Bordel and Sharpe's	Michael White	320
94.	Richmond	Patrick Cruickshank	500
95.	Richmond Vale <u>or</u> Fitzhughes	Thomas Fitzhugh	388
96.	Rose Bank	Devisees of George Dalzell and Joseph W. Mayer, deceased	250
97.	Wallilabo	Devisees of John Grant and Lewis Grant, deceased	500
		(E) Sub-Total	4,070

(F) ISLAND OF BEQUIA

98.	Belmont	W.T. Dickenson	105
99.	Friendship	Devisees of Charles John Warner, deceased	483
100.	Hope	Devisees of John Henderson	300
101.	Industry	William T. Dickerson	1,000
102.	Mt. Pleasant	Devisees of Peter Audain and Mrs. Herries	200
103.	Paget Farm	William Stowe	220
104.	Reform	Mons. Marricheau and others	200
105.	Spring:	William Rose Scott, Thomas Scott and Walter Scott, ½; the Devisees of Charles Warner, ½	619
106.	Union	William Rose	206
		(F) Sub-Total	3,693

(G) ISLAND OF MUSTIQUE

107.	Cheltenham	Christopher Punnett	683
108.	Adelphi	Messrs Trimminghams	1,992
		(G) Sub-Total	2,675

(H) ISLAND OF CANOUAN

109.	Carenage	Mrs. Snagg	600

(I) UNION ISLAND

110.	Union Island	Devisees of Samuel Span	2,057
		GRAND TOTAL	44,798 acres

SOURCE: Charles Shepherd: *An Historical Account of the Island of Saint Vincent* (First Published in London, 1831; Republished by Frank Cass and Co. Limited, London, 1997).

Appendix 4

Summary of Embarked/Disembarked Slaves –
St. Vincent and the Grenadines as Principal Place of Landing

YEAR	EMBARKED	DISEMBARKED
1764 – 1765	205	167
1766 – 1770	3,108	2,509
1771 – 1775	10,872	9,219
1776 – 1780	564	517
1781 – 1785	4,372	3,893
1786 – 1790	11,711	10,532
1791 – 1795	14,426	13,652
1796 – 1800	7,743	6,820
1801 – 1805	7,062	6,375
1806 – 1808	2,113	1,878
Totals	62,176	55,562

SOURCE: *The Slave Trade Database* by Emory University et al (2013).

NOTES: The trade in slaves in British ships and to British colonies was formally abolished in 1807.

Between 1779 and 1783 France temporarily took control of St. Vincent.

Joseph Spinelli in his 1973 doctoral dissertation *Land Use and Population in St. Vincent, 1763-1960*, in utilising data from the Estates Books and other sources, informs us that in 1812 there were 24,920 slaves in St. Vincent and the Grenadines; in 1832, the number of registered slaves stood at 22,997; and in 1833, the last full year of slavery, there were 18,794 slaves. Spinelli proffers the explanation for the decline in numbers of slaves as follows:

> The attrition in numbers of slaves was the result of the higher mortality of an aging, predominantly male population without sufficient reproduction to compensate for deaths and the periodic manumission of the elderly and infirm from the slave registers.

III.
A Review Essay of Hilary Beckles' *Britain's Black Debt: Reparations for Caribbean Slavery And Native Genocide*

Presented at the Book Launch on May 02, 2013, at Kingston, Jamaica, sponsored by the University of the West Indies Press

Author's Note: St. Vincent and the Grenadines is hosting a Regional Conference on Reparations between Sunday, September 15th and Tuesday, September 17th, 2013. As a contribution to the on-going discussions on Reparations on the eve of the Conference, I cause to be published a Review Essay of Professor Hilary Beckles' book on the subject. This Review Essay provides an overview of Beckles' book and integrated other material into the narrative. This Review Essay was first presented in Jamaica on May 02, 2013, when Professor Beckles' book was launched.

Introduction

Professor Sir Hilary Mc. D. Beckles, Principal of the Cave Hill Campus of the University of the West Indies, has authored a path-breaking book entitled *Britain's Black Debt: Reparations for Caribbean Slavery and Native Genocide*. It was published earlier this year by the University of the West Indies Press of Mona, Kingston, Jamaica.

This 292-page volume is conveniently divided into two parts: Part I introduces the discussion of the principles and politics of reparations and lays out the relevant historical data which ground the demand for reparations; Part II carefully examines the case for reparations and details the meandering fate of the reparations movement in recent years.

Beckles writes in a refreshing, compelling style; his narrative conveys the hard-nosed historian's affinity for facts from which truths are inexorably derived; his conceptual clarity on the subject of reparations for slavery and native genocide reflects a razor-sharp mind which is among the best globally in his business, his trade, of historical research and writing. On the subject matters at hand, Beckles writes with commitment to truth and justice; he evinces, too, a passionate intensity which brings out the best in a seasoned child of our Caribbean civilisation, not as a propagandist but as an experienced student of Caribbean historiography who has a duty to speak for his native antecedents and enslaved forbears and to seek just recompense for their descendants. To borrow the language of George Lamming, our revered seer and creative genius, Beckles glows with a brightness which is illuminating, not blinding. Everton Weekes was cricket's master craftsman with whom Beckles collaborated in his autobiography. Beckles, in his *Britain's Black Debt* puts on a display of self-mastery in seeking to right historical wrongs which confirms him as the Caribbean's most scholarly, impressive and influential public intellectual.

Beckles' book which we are launching this evening is a multi-disciplinary masterpiece: It is history, philosophy, political economy, cultural authoritativeness, international jurisprudence, and literature of the creative imagination. Its analyses are wide and deep, particular and general; the book touches both the individual and the collective in a gripping manner which connects tellingly with the mind and the spirit. The significance of this book cannot be overstated: It is historical writing of the highest quality; it is most valuable for public education and the process of popular conscientisation; and it is a foundation-stone for coordinated public policy in the Caribbean to advance the claim, formally, for reparations.

To be sure, much of the actual data in Beckles' book is already available elsewhere but he marshals known information with freshness and additional insight in the specific service of the case for reparations. Still, though, abundant new data have been assembled to bolster further the historical and contemporary demand for appropriate recompense for Caribbean slavery and native genocide.

From the outset, Beckles makes it plain that he is not on an anti-British crusade in his quest for reparations from Britain for its central role in the crimes of slavery and native genocide in Britain's Caribbean colonies. Explicitly, Beckles states:

> The Caribbean reparation case against Britain is not based on any concept or intention to participate in political confrontation with the British society or its government. A confrontational approach to reparation does not hold reconciliation as a primary objective. Reconciliation, however, is the necessary outcome of the claim for reparations, seeking as it does to establish a spirit of mutual respect and obligation between the British state and the descendants of enslaved Africans who continued to be victimized a century after legislative emancipation in 1838.
>
> ...It is important for British society to acknowledge that its development as a nation-state, the transformation of its economy to sustainable industrialization, and its global standing as a super power among nations were founded upon a crime against humanity in a form of racial chattel enslavement of African bodies and the global trafficking of millions of these bodies for three hundred years.
>
> Acknowledging and accounting for wrongs is deeply enshrined in British law and society. And as such, the need to engage British society with a reparations discourse is consistent with national, cultural and intellectual norms. Indeed, the British intellectual and moral traditions should insist upon it. Far from seeing reparations claims as confrontational, then, British society should champion the cause as an expression of respect and of celebration of the finest aspects of its judicial culture.

So, the quest is not for confrontation. Nevertheless, the case for reparations has to be made as robustly as the circumstances demand. The unanswerable case has to be grounded in historical and contemporary facts, morality, politics, and law. Our people and governments must be mobilized in unity, in a massive campaign, on the matter. We must galvanise all possible allies in this great cause, cognizant of the fact that no great cause has ever been won by doubtful men and women. Our overall strategy and tactics must be impeccable and in accordance with international norms. We must act with urgency, yet be patient because it is, and will be, a rough, hard road to travel even though justice is on our side. Beckles' book highlights all this, and more, in its advisories.

Exterminate the Savages: Genocide in the Windwards

Hilary Beckles devotes one chapter of his book explicitly on the subject of native genocide under the eye-catching heading, "Exterminate the Savages: Genocide in the Windwards". Succinctly, and compellingly, Beckles states the core of the issue, thus:

> The English entered the Eastern Caribbean in the early seventeenth century with a colonizing policy based on violent land appropriation and dispossession of the indigenous population. The use of military power to defeat native communities was matched with a mentality that made possible their extermination when met with resistance. At the outset, the natives were considered undesirable and dispensable. War was unleashed upon these communities with a view to seizing their land and labour. If they could be enslaved, then the added bonus was welcomed. The English state sanctioned this policy and financed its operations. State and private sectors joined together in the hope of massive material reward.

Beckles provides chapter and verse to substantiate each limb of these conclusions. In the first phase of conquest, extirpation of the natives, and attempted settlement by the English, the native population in the Lesser Antilles fell between 1492 and 1730 by as much as 90 percent, according to the distinguished English historian of the Caribbean, Michael Craton. After 1730, and more particularly after the conclusion of the Seven Years War and the accompanying Treaty of Paris in 1763 between the French and the English, the extent of the genocide against all native peoples became even more ferocious.

The native populations were variously described as "Indians", "Caribs", sometimes Arawaks, and in countries such as Dominica, St. Vincent, and the Leeward Islands they called themselves "Kalinagos" (also spelt Calinagos), whom others later labeled as "Yellow Caribs". From the late seventeenth century fully into the eighteenth century in St. Vincent and the Grenadines, the off-spring of the Kalinagos and Africans (runaways from neighboring Barbados and survivors from a shipwreck in 1670) became known as the Garifuna (also spelt Karifuna) and constituted the majority of the population until African slaves in large numbers were forcibly taken from West Africa between 1764 and 1807 to man the sugar plantation economy. The colonialists called the Garifuna, "Black Caribs".

In every island in the Lesser Antilles, the Kalinagos, and later the Garifuna people defended their lands, their patrimony, from European encroachment and aggression. From time to time, the native populations adopted flexible tactics which involved negotiations and active resistance. For example, on March 23, 1667, Kalinago leaders of St. Vincent, Dominica, and St. Lucia met with an English delegation headed by the Governor of Barbados, William Lord Willoughby, in St. Vincent to negotiate peace. At the signing of the Treaty were Anmwatta, (the Grand Babba or Chief of all Kalinagos), Chiefs Wappya, Nay, Le Suroe, Rebura and Aloons. A one-sided Treaty was signed which gave the English essentially all they wanted: Suzerainty over the island; loyalty of the Kalinagos to the King of England; and the return to Barbados of any African slave or other fugitive who fled that British colony.

Willoughby intended to use the treaty as a spring-board for settlement of these islands for sugar production. Within two months of the Kalinago-Willoughby Treaty, a party of fifty-four English colonists from Barbados arrived in St. Vincent to start-up the settlement. The Kalinagos, the Garifunas, and the Africans resisted their presence and drove them from the island. In response, Willoughby unleashed a full-scale genocidal offensive. The Kalinagos and their allies rebuffed Willoughby's expedition, it having suffered heavy losses.

Constant skirmishes and war took their toll on the Kalinagos. According to the priest-observer, Pére Jean-Baptiste Labat, by 1770, adult Kalinagos in St. Vincent and Dominica did not exceed 2000. Still, their militancy and the rugged terrain of these islands restrained potential English settlers. By then, too, the Garifuna constituted a clear majority of the population, certainly in St. Vincent. They, indeed, had become hardened guerilla fighters under their Chief, Joseph Chatoyer.

So, by the time of the Treaty of Paris in 1763, in a general Anglo-French carve-up of West Indian territories, Britain was allocated St. Vincent, Grenada, St. Lucia and Tobago. They had already settled Barbados, St. Kitts, Nevis, and Antigua in the Lesser Antilles. But by then the Kalinago nation was broken, through the British policy of genocide against them. So, I pose this query of relevance which Beckles himself has sharply raised: Given that the extermination of the Kalinagos had anticipated a similar later treatment of the Maori tribes in Australia, how is it that Queen Elizabeth II of Great Britain had offered an official apology for that acknowledged crime against humanity, and her government paid reparations accordingly, but nothing in these respects has been offered and done for the descendants of the Kalinagos and their nation-states of St. Vincent, Dominica, Grenada, St. Lucia and the Leeward Islands (St. Kitts-Nevis, Antigua-Barbuda)?

Beckles is emphatic on reparations for native genocide. He correctly observes in his book:

> The colonization of three-quarters of the world's people and places by western European nations created rich opportunities for (such) crimes (against humanity) to flourish. In the Caribbean context, the genocide against the indigenous populations, the sexual plunder of their women by imperial soldiers and the appropriation of their wealth by merchants and military leaders preceded the mass enslavement of Africans. Such crimes have had lasting and damaging effects in the psychological, material and social conditions of those victimized and on generations of their progeny.

In a paper recently authored and published by me entitled "Preliminary Notes on the Quantification of Reparations from the British For Lands Stolen, For Genocide, For Forcible Deportation of the Garifuna People, and For Enslavement of Africans in St. Vincent and the Grenadines",

I have traced the contours and some specifics of all these issues in the period 1763 to 1834, from the assumption of suzerainty by the British for St. Vincent and the Grenadines to the formal emancipation of slaves.

One of the first acts of the British colonizers in 1764 was to declare that all lands in St. Vincent and the Grenadines belonged to the British Crown. At one stroke they deprived the Garifuna and the Kalinago people of all their land which was held in common, save and except for under 2000 acres which the natives had allowed French settlers to occupy and cultivate on the western side of St. Vincent. Please note that St. Vincent and the Grenadines admeasures 150 square miles or some 96,000 acres of land (85,120 acres on St. Vincent; and 10,880 acres in the Grenadines).

From 1764 to 1795, the Garifuna/Kalinago nation fought the British colonizers. The land issue was central to the popular native resistance to British colonisation. Bit-by-bit, chunk-by-chunk, the British took the lands of the Garifuna/Kalinago people on one pretext after another. The British finally defeated the Garifuna/Kalinago people in 1795 and in subsequent skirmishes. On March 14, 1795, a British ambush and massacre of the Garifuna patriots occasioned the death of the Paramount Chief Joseph Chatoyer. As part of our nation's historical reclamation, my government formally declared the Right Excellent Joseph Chatoyer as the First National Hero of St. Vincent and the Grenadines on March 14, 2002.

By 1800, the Garifuna/Kalinago people were practically quarantined on an allocated parcel of 238 acres of land in an inaccessible area of the north-east of St. Vincent. Thus, between 1763 and 1800, a mere 37 years, the Garifuna/Kalinago people lost the remainder of their 85,120 acres of land on St. Vincent and the 10,800 acres in the Grenadines. In 1804, the Garifuna were legally barred from owning their land. The British government must pay for these lands from which the British Treasury and its grantees benefitted directly to the detriment of the Garifuna/Kalinago nation and their successors in independent St. Vincent and the Grenadines. For example, in 1764, the British government auctioned 20,538 acres of land on St. Vincent. On this sale, the British Treasury earned directly £162,854, an average of £7.16 shillings per acre. Using a conservative factor of 900 to put the 1764 values in those of 2013, this figure amounts to £146.59 million today or EC $612.7 million.

In 1764, the British government granted to General Robert Monckton, a "hero" of the Seven Years' War, 4,000 acres of land on the Windward coast of St. Vincent. Monckton promptly sold the land for £30,000 or £27.0 million (EC $112.9 million) in today's value. Similarly, in 1777 the British Government granted Lt. Colonel George Etherington a huge parcel of land on the northwest of St. Vincent on account of his services to the British in the American War of Independence. Like-wise for an identical reason, Colonel Thomas Brown was granted 6,000 acres of former "Carib Country" lands in 1807 valued then at £135,000 or £114.75 million (EC $479.7 million) in today's value.

Why did the British not grant Monckton, Etherington and Brown, lands in London, Cambridge, Oxford or Liverpool for services to the British Crown? Why give them land in St. Vincent and the Grenadines? They had only done disservice to the native population.

It is estimated by me that the 64,000 acres of land which the British "stole" from the Garifuna/Kalinago nation in St. Vincent and the Grenadines is assessed in today's value at £918 million or EC$3.84 billion.

Regarding the assessment for genocide of the Garifuna/Kalinago people at the years 1795-1797, the following numbers are relevant: Native population, 9,000 in 1795; estimated number killed in war or slaughtered immediately thereafter, 2,500; actual number who died on an inhospitable, offshore island of Balliceaux awaiting forcible deportation, 2,445; actual number forcibly exiled in 1797 to Central America, 2,026. Thus, less than 2,000 Garifuna/Kalinago survived in St. Vincent after British genocide and forced exile. As such, therefore, the British exterminated from St. Vincent through genocide (5,167 persons) and forced deportation (2,026) or some 7,193 Garifuna people...80 percent of the Garifuna nation on St. Vincent. These are horrendous statistics of an incredible, historic crime of genocide for which the British must pay appropriate recompense to the nation of St. Vincent and the Grenadines, including the descendants of the Garifuna/Kalinago people.

Interestingly, the British had also forcibly deported rebels from the Tacky revolt in Jamaica in the late eighteenth century and from the Fedon Rebellion in Grenada in 1795 to the Bay of Honduras in Central America.

Beckles fittingly, and accurately, concludes his narrative on native genocide in the following terms:

> By refusing to capitulate under the collective military pressure of Europeans, however, the Kalinagos and then the Karifunas, had kept the Windward Islands in a marginal relation to the slave plantation complex for two hundred years, and in so doing made a principal contribution to the freedom traditions of the Caribbean. This history speaks to the origins and legacy of the British official policy of genocide in the Caribbean. The native community experienced the full impact of the policy. Survivors today struggle to sustain what is left of their "nation". Defeated in battle, scattered and politically marginalised, victims continue their rebuilding efforts. They have a legal right to reparations claims. No legal claim is clearer. Only political will and community organization are required to present the case.

The History of Slavery in the Caribbean

In nine chapters of his book, Professor Beckles meticulously documents the historiography of the slave trade, slavery, emancipation, and the payment of reparations to the slave owners. The chapter headings point to the focus of his analysis:

> King James' Version: Royal Caribbean Slave Voyages
> Not Human: Britain's Black Property
> The "Zong" Massacre: Jamaica Bound Africans Murdered
>
> Prostituting Enslaved Caribbean Women
> Criminal Enrichment: Building Britain with Slavery
> Dividends from the Devil: Church of England Chattels in Barbados
> Earls of Harewood: Slave Route to Buckingham Palace
> Slave Owners in Parliament and the Private Sector
> Twenty Million Pounds: Slave Owners' Reparations.

Each of these chapters is riveting reading with an abundance of new material and well-known data refreshingly presented.

Beckles opens his discussion on the slave trade and African enslavement with a majestic paragraph and provides detailed support thereafter. Thus, he tellingly summarises:

> The British obtained Africans for enslavement and transatlantic trading by all means possible, including widespread kidnapping, and destroying states that opposed them and assassinating their political leaders. During the middle of the sixteenth century, when they began formally to participate in the selling of enchained African bodies across the Atlantic, it was understood in England as a criminal commerce, and slave merchants knew it to be so.

From the beginning to the end of the slave trade and slavery, the British state was intimately involved with this global commercial enterprise, hand-in-glove with the private sector, other non-governmental institutions in Britain, and the society as a whole. It was truly a national endeavour without moral scruples designed to enrich the British, especially its ruling and governing classes in real property, banking and finance, insurance, shipping and ship-building, manufacturing, wholesale and retail trade, and commerce generally. The cities of London, Bristol, and Liverpool, for example were enriched by the triangular trade, led by Britain, between Britain, Africa, and the Caribbean.

The British state provided the military muscle, through its army and navy, to support its nefarious global commercial enterprise in the slave trade and the enslavement of Africans in the Caribbean, and elsewhere. The British state enacted the laws, including racist, social, governance, property and shipping laws, underpinning slavery and the slave trade. It marshaled together an entire cultural and intellectual edifice, including a racist ideology, to justify the slave trade, and slavery, and to legitimate all those who engaged in the enchainment of Africans in Africa and the New World. The Church of England, philosophers, politicians, and popular commentators bolstered the British state's criminal public policy. All of this, and more, Professor Beckles provides data, insights, and analyses to explain, guide, and educate, in the service of truth and justice, and the quest for reparations.

Beckles begins his historical journey with the four slave-trading voyages of John Hawkins between 1562 and 1568; traces the explosion in the slave trade from the mid-1650s onwards until the abolition of the slave trade in 1807; maps the settlement of the earlier British colonies of Barbados, St. Kitts, Nevis, Antigua, and then Jamaica (after 1655) unto the later settlement of the Windward Islands, Trinidad, and Guiana... all with the slave mode of production, imposed by mercantile capitalism, which slavery itself was contributing immensely to metamorphose into industrial capitalism; explains the transformation of Caribbean societies as the plantation economy based on sugar, including the marked alterations in the production apparatuses, the increased generation of wealth and profits for planters and merchants, and the consolidation of slavery; takes us through the twists and turns leading to abolition of the slave trade in 1807, the legal emancipation of slaves in 1834, and the apprenticeship system, 1834-1838.

In the process of this historical journey, Beckles' well-honed multi-disciplinary skills and acute judgments are on amazing display. They constitute in him a veritable noise in his blood, an echo in his bones, to borrow and adapt a Maroon expression from Jamaica. Along the way Beckles brings into the narrative the relevance and impact of the political evolution in Britain; the alterations over time of the nature of Britain capitalism; the American War of Independence; the extraordinary and special case of Haiti; the role of important personalities, institutions, and firms in Britain, African, and the Caribbean; and the changing socio-economic and political condition in the Caribbean, including the sharp resistance of the slaves themselves to slavery.

In his historical journey, Professor Beckles weaves the various contending interpretations in Caribbean historiography of seminal events. For example, on the matter of the weight to be assigned to various factors in the unfolding of slavery's emancipation, he evaluates the role of the British abolitionists, the changing political circumstances in Britain, including the battle for political reform generally, the resistance of the slaves, and the altered nature of Britain's capitalism. Convincingly, Beckles opts for the historical, materialist thesis, first advanced by C. L. R James in *Black Jacobins* and fleshed out thoroughly in Eric Williams' *Capitalism and Slavery*, that Caribbean slavery which was a child of mercantile capitalism and had fuelled its expansion into industrial capitalism but had by the early nineteenth century become a brake on the further expansion of industrial capitalism itself. Thus, slavery had to go; it had become comparatively uneconomic for an advancing industrial capitalism.

Beckles embraces, too, as a companion to the historical materialist thrust of the Williams Thesis, the dialectical materialist perspective of Richard Hart established in his book *Slaves Who Abolished Slavery*. The class, and racial, contradictions between the slaves and the planter-merchant elite generated anti-slavery resistance in various ways on an on-going basis and erupted, from time to time, in large scale uprisings or revolts. History records in Kenneth Morgan's *Slavery and the British Empire* that between 1638, when a general slave rebellion broke out on Providence Island in the Bahamas, *and* 1837, when a mutiny occurred among the First West Indian Regiment in Trinidad, there were seventeen slave revolts in the British Caribbean that involved dozens of slaves, thirty-eight acts of *collective* resistance with hundreds of slaves, fifteen outbreaks of violence with thousands of slaves, and five rebellions that included many thousands of slaves. The major slave uprisings were Tacky's Rebellion in western Jamaica in 1760; Julian Fédon's rebellion in Grenada in 1795 – 1796; (Fédon was a "free coloured" planter who mobilized the slaves and free coloureds against the Anglophone whites); the Bussa Revolt in Barbados in 1816 in which Nanny Grigg, a literate domestic slave, also played an important role; the Demerara revolt in 1823 of which Quamina, a senior deacon at Bethel Chapel, assumed the figurehead role; and Sam Sharpe's Christmas rebellion of 1831–32 in Jamaica. In Haiti, there was the extraordinary popular Slave Revolution led by Toussaint L'Ouverture in 1791; and the Garifuna Resistance in the Windward Islands.

Professor Beckles, of course, credits abolitionists, including those steeped in humane religious beliefs, and political reformers in Britain, with pushing the legislative agenda for slavery's formal abolition in the British Parliament. Still, the context of slavery's restraint on the further expansion of capitalism and the slave's resistance to enslavement were fundamental.

In this regard, I am reminded of the insights offered by Karl Marx in his brilliant work entitled *The Eighteenth Brumaire of Louis Napoleon* published in 1869:

Men make their own history, but they do not make it just as they please; they do not make it under circumstances chosen by themselves, but under circumstances directly encountered, given and transmitted from the past. The tradition of all the dead generations weighs like a nightmare on the brain of the living.

In *Black Jacobins*, C. L. R James makes a similar, profound point:

Great men make history but only such history as is it is possible for them to make. Their freedom of achievement is limited by the necessities of their environment. To portray the limits of those necessities and the realization, complete or partial, of all the possibilities, that is the true business of the historian.

From the standpoint of reparations for African enslavement, it does not matter greatly on what side of "causation debate" in respect of the abolition of the slave trade and slavery that one comes down. What is vital is to grasp the criminal and inhumane nature of the slave trade and slavery, the immense contribution of slavery and the West Indian colonies to the British economy, and the unanswerable case for reparations.

Beckles correctly advises that "the Middle Passage" did not begin with the actual transatlantic voyage on a slave-trader's vessel, but rather with the capture of Africans in the interior of Africa; and it ended with their adjustment experience in the Americas, including the Caribbean. Beckles identifies six distinct stages of the Middle Passage: (i) Capture and enslavement in Africa; (ii) the journey to the coast and other departure points; (iii) the storage and packaging for shipment; (iv) the transatlantic crossing; (v) sale and dispersion in the Americas and Caribbean; (vi) adjustments in the Americas, including the Caribbean. Each stage was a horrific, inhuman experience. Beckles provides us with telling, heart-rending, yet sobering, details.

Importantly, Beckles authoritatively rubbishes the jaundiced and historically-incorrect assertions by some commentators that Africans sold Africans into slavery and thus are equally culpable as the Europeans for the horrendous slave trade. To be sure, some Africans seized others for enslavement but such seizures were systematically encouraged by the British; it was, more often than not, a case of seize or be seized. The

British actually subverted chieftains and states in Africa who baulked at this criminal trade in human bodies. Moreover, the British traders actively organized raids and seizures. Further, it was the British state which built forts and holding areas for slaves across West Africa. The British, too, were the owners and operators of the ships. To the extent that some Africans cooperated with the British it was marginal and incidental. In any event, in any society, there are always itinerant hustlers and individuals who prey on others' misfortunes or weaknesses. Do such hustlers or native criminal entrepreneurs define their societies? Not at all! The British state and society fully organised and endorsed the enslavement of Africans for the Americas. They are wholly responsible!

Moreover, Africans resisted their capture and enslavement, often violently, on the ground in Africa and upon their forced boarding of the slave ships. Such resistance continued on the slave ships themselves. Beckles provides the historical data to support all this.

An interesting, supporting perspective comes from a slave-trader, the captain of slave vessel turned Minister of the gospel, John Newton, in a 1788 publication entitled *Thoughts on the African Slave Trade: A Memoir of my Infidel Days as a Slaving Captain*:

> Slaves are the staple article of the traffic, and though a considerable number may have been born near the sea, I believe the bulk of them are acquired from afar. I have reason to think that some travel more than a thousand miles before they reach the sea coast. Whether there may be convicts among these likewise, or what proportion they may bear to those who are taken as prisoners of war, it is impossible to know, but I judge the principal source of slaves to be the wars which prevail among the natives. ...I verily believe that the far greater part of the wars in Africa would cease if the Europeans would cease to tempt them by offering goods for slaves.

It is undeniable that the transatlantic crossing for the slaves was inhumane and horrible in the extreme. There were discourses about which method of packing them in below the deck of the ships was more advantageous to the traders: "Loose packing" or "tight packing". Murder, rape, cruel and inhuman punishment, inadequate feeding, cramped survival conditions, filth and awful stench, attended the slaves on the voyages to the Caribbean and the Americas. Mortality among the slaves was as high as 20 percent in the seventeenth and eighteenth centuries but had dropped to roughly five percent in the nineteenth century. In the case of St. Vincent, between 1764 and 1807, 62,176 slaves embarked for that country on 240 voyages, and 55,562 arrived; thus, there was an aggregate loss on these voyages of 11 percent.

Historians of all stripes have documented the horror of slavery in the Caribbean for the slaves physically, culturally, psychologically, economically, legally, and politically. They were legally defined as "chattels", as property with no human rights. Economic and racist oppression was beyond the worst kind imaginable. Beckles is excellent in his description of all this.

The story of slavery's inhumanity is well-known from historians of yesterday and today. So, let us take the account of a slave published in 1831 entitled *The History of Mary Prince: A West Indian Slave, Related by Herself*:

> I am often vexed, and I feel great sorrow when I hear some people in this country say, that the slaves do not need better usage, and do not want to be free.... I say, Not so. How can slaves be happy when they have the halter around their neck and the whip upon their back and are disgraced and thought no more of than beasts...and are separated from their mothers, and husbands, and children, and sisters, just as cattle are sold and separated? Is it happiness for a driver in the field to take down his wife or sister or child, and strip them, and whip them in such a disgraceful manner...women that have had children exposed in the open field to shame?! There is no modesty or decency shown by the owner to his slaves.... They tie them up like hogs... moor them up like cattle, and they lick them, so as hogs, or cattle, or horses never were flogged; and yet they come home (to England) and say, and make some good people believe, that slaves don't want to get out of slavery. But they put a cloak about the truth.... We don't mind hard work, if we had proper treatment and proper wages like English servants, and proper time given in the week to keep us from breaking the Sabbath. But they won't give it; they will have

work-work-work, night and day, sick and well, till we are done up; and we must not speak nor look amiss, however much we be abused. And then when we are quite done up, who cares for us, more than for a lame horse? This is slavery.

Beckles is correctly emphatic that the three million enchained Africans whom the English shipped across to the Caribbean were the basis of Britain's expanded empire. Its leading economic enterprise at the end of the eighteenth century was Jamaica. After the Haitian Revolution and the defeat of the French by "the Black Jacobins", the English were left with the status as lead Caribbean enslaver...a nation in possession of nearly four million "chattels", slaves!

Caribbean slavery adversely affected population growth; it was a direct consequence of slavery's criminality. Professor Beckles instructs us accordingly:

> The cruelty and brutality of the labour system subverted any potential for the enslaved African population to reproduce. Jamaica was a demographic disaster for enslaved Africans. For British enslavers, the colony was the land of opportunity. It had replaced Barbados as the most profitable colony but did not succeed in growing the enslaved population naturally as Barbados had done. Plantation records speak to the human catastrophe of slavery. In Barbados, the first slave society and England's largest slave-investment project, English crimes against humanity were staged on the broadest scale.

In St. Vincent and the Grenadines, 55,562 slaves, on 240 voyages, arrived from Africa between 1764 and 1807. But by 1832, the last year of slave registration, there were 22,997 slaves. Harsh treatment of slaves, a high mortality rate, and an aging, predominantly male population without a sufficiency of reproduction to compensate for the deaths and the periodic manumission of the infirm and elderly, occasioned the population decline of the enslaved.

The British abolitionist and esteemed poet, William Cowper, lyrically sums up the slaves' condition in the first two verses of a veritable abolitionist anthem, *The Negro's Complaint,* written in 1786, published in 1793:

> Forc'd from home and all its pleasures,
> Afric's coast I left forlorn.
> To increase a stranger's treasures,
> O'er the raging billows borne.
> Men from England bought and sold me,
> Paid my price in paltry gold;
> But, though slave they have enrolled me,
> Minds are never to be sold.
> "Still in thought as free as ever,
> What are England's rights I ask,
> Me from my delights to sever,
> Me to torture, me to task?
> Fleecy locks, and black complexion
> Cannot forfeit nature's claim;
> Skins may differ, but affection
> Dwells in white and black the same.

Criminal Enrichment: Building Britain with Slavery

Undoubtedly, Britain was the beneficiary of criminal enrichment through the slave trade, slavery, and its Caribbean colonies. It is surely unquestionable that African slavery in the Caribbean contributed immensely to the building of Britain's economy.

Professor Beckles tackles this vital issue in this summary way:

> All Western European nations participated in the traffic in enchained African bodies and reaped the benefits that the enslavement of these bodies conferred on investors. But the British reaped the lion's share and, more than any other European nation, perfected the economic and financial art of exploiting the African. By the end of the eighteenth century, Britain was the

slave-trading nation par excellence and the primary Caribbean enslaver. On both fronts, then...slave trafficking and slave driving...the British ruled supreme.

Beckles further informs us that:

> More enslaved Africans suffered at British hands in the Caribbean than at the hands of any other colonial power. British hegemony in the slave trade and its ownership of Jamaica, the largest slave economy in the region in 1800, established the nation as the market leader and trend setter. Some three million Africans were shipped out of Africa during the eighteenth century in British ships, twice the number of other nations. The British thus established their status as the nation with the greatest capacity to remove African inhabitants forcibly from their homes and relocate them finally elsewhere.

In 1692, Sir Joshua Child, economist and English nationalist, authored and caused to be published a book entitled: *A New Discourse on Trade*. He measured the Caribbean's value to England in terms of the wealth repatriated to generate employment, and the market for English manufacturers. Child concluded that, in the seventeenth century, Barbados was worth more to England than all the American colonies combined; Barbados was the heart of English slavery. Child's view was that the Caribbean had become the most precious group of colonies ever recorded.

Beckles reports that by 1775, the British West Indies plantations were valued at £50 million (£71.7 billion in 2010 values); only three years later they were estimated to be worth £70 million (£97.9 billion in 2010 values).

Accordingly, Professor Beckles opines that:

> The Caribbean market was the principal site for this rush to riches. Barbados, defined in the seventeenth century as 'the brightest jewel in His Majesty's crown', was the largest market; it was surpassed by Jamaica early in the eighteenth century. The 'guinney trade', as it was called, worked 'to the national advantage'

and its influence could be felt everywhere, from Parliament to Palace, from the seat of government to the ghettoes around it. It was a feast on the flesh of enchained Africans.

Beckles quotes the authoritative James A. Rawley in his book *The Transatlantic Slave Trade: A History (New York, Nation, 1981)*:

> In the decade of the 1750s England had become the supreme slavery nation in the Atlantic World, a standing she occupied until 1807 [when the slave trade was abolished]. In the period from 1751 to 1800 England exported 42 percent of the slaves taken from Africa; 52 percent in the years from 1791 to 1807. England's annual export of slaves rose from about 7,000 in the late seventeenth century to twice that figure in the 1740s, to nearly 40,000 in the late years of the eighteenth century.

It is well-established that "enslaved African bodies" served as a "cash cow" for most British port, towns and cities, through the eighteenth century. Bristol, Liverpool, London and Glasgow were pre-eminent. Beckles piles on the evidence in support of all this, and more. Before him Eric Williams in *Capitalism and Slavery*, and other economic historians, had amply demonstrated this. Those who have contended otherwise have done so on spurious evidence and counter-factual theorising. Beckles takes on the lot of these critics including P.R. O'Brien, David Eltis, Stanley Engerman, and Kenneth Morgan, and prevails most persuasively and conclusively. He does so brilliantly with the help of economic historians who are of a like-mind such as Barbara Solow, William Darity, Robin Blackburn, Gavin Wright, Jacob Price, and J.E. Irihori. This section of Beckles' *Britain's Black Debt* is vital to the reparations cause.

Support, too, even if qualified somewhat, has come from David B. Ryden's *West Indian Slavery and British Abolition, 1783-1807* (Cambridge University Press, 2009). Ryden considers that J.E. Irihori in his book, *Africans and the Industrial Revolution in England: A Study in International Trade and Development* (Cambridge University Press, 2002), has compiled the most empirical evidence, supportive of Williams' *Capitalism and Slavery* in two respects: (i) To demonstrate the significant role the slave trade played in the capital accumulation in England; and (ii) to stake out the claim that the slave-fueled economic growth in the Americas was a vital component to Britain's industrial growth.

Let us leave the final words on this subject to Barbara Solow and Hilary Beckles. In her essay "Capitalism and Slavery in the Exceedingly Long Run" published in Barbara L. Solow and Stanley L. Engerman (ed.), *British Capitalism and Caribbean Slavery: The Legacy of Eric Williams* (Cambridge University Press, 1987), Solow persuasively argues that:

> The importance of Caribbean slavery to British growth depended on particular circumstances and was confined to a particular historical period.... (The Caribbean economy) based on slavery benefitted Britain when investment was lagging, technical change was slow, growth in domestic demand for manufacture was less than in external demand, and when the North American colonies depended on Britain for manufacture and the West Indies for foreign exchange with which to buy them.

Magisterially, Professor Beckles concludes:

> To acknowledge, then, the role of the Caribbean in fostering Britain's economic development in the seventeenth and eighteenth centuries is to examine honestly the relations between an imperial country and the colonies it created for purposes of commercial exploitation. The Caribbean slave complex, as Solow tells us, was the principal source of the 'foreign exchange' for the North American colonies owned by Britain, and later by the imperial centre itself. To argue that slavery was important for economic growth is not to claim that slavery caused the Industrial Revolution. She (Solow) concludes: "Slavery did not cause the Industrial Revolution, but played an active role in its pattern and timing'. By the 1820s, when Britain was a self-sustaining industrial nation, 'the West Indies mattered less." It had served its purposes. It was time to put it aside and move on.

Some Institutions, Personalities, Families, and Companies in the Slave Enterprise in the Caribbean

Although the British state was intimately entwined in every aspect of the slave trade and slavery in its West Indian colonies, it was a bundle of institutions, individuals, families, and companies, enmeshed with, and within, the colonial state apparatus, which conjointly acted in accordance with the State colonial policy, and all profited from it.

A major institution which supported slavery was the Church of England. Beckles is forthright about its role in his book:

> The Church of England, represented by its Anglican clergy that spread across the Caribbean throughout the seventeenth and eighteenth centuries, took centre stage as an important player in the slave-based economy. Its relationship to the enslaved was neither pastoral nor spiritual, but financial and entrepreneurial. The clergy engaged in the important ideological work of defending African enslavement. It blessed slave traders and slave ships, and presided over events such as executions of the rebellious. Critically, the clergy were elite private investors in slave plantations which they owned and managed.

Across the British West Indies, from Anguilla and the Virgin Islands down the entire chain of colonies to Guiana, there were 128 members of the clergy who were recipients of compensation for owning enslaved Africans; sixty-two of the clergy were in Jamaica; twenty in Barbados; sixteen in Antigua; and six in St. Vincent.

The conduct of Anglican bishops and priests in the West Indies during slavery was surely not in keeping with the teachings of Christ. Beckles again provides abundant details of their unacceptable conduct. Meanwhile, most clergy from the Methodists, Baptists, and Moravians were at work daily to facilitate amelioration in the slaves' condition and to prepare them for their earliest possible freedom. Still, it must be said that outstanding members of the Anglican laity, including William Wilberforce, agitated on behalf of the slaves, first for an end to the slave-trade and then for slavery's termination itself.

In England, a society was founded under the name of the London Society of West Indian Planters and Merchants (known popularly as "the Society") which was an organising centre for anti-abolition activities. The most important personalities in the society were linked to Jamaica, and their lobbying efforts for slavery were extensive and intensive.

In his book, *West Indian Slavery and Abolition, 1783–1807*, David B. Ryden informs us that:

> The political power of the Jamaican planter reached its height during the late eighteenth century. Buoyed by climbing European sugar prices in the 1790s, the island's political and economic elite left the colony for Britain in increasing numbers, where the prototypical absentee split his time between an exclusive London residence and a manor home in rural Britain. The private wealth derived from slave labour was extraordinary and afforded a select few a sumptuous life style. Men such as Simon Taylor, James Pinnock, William Chisholme, Philip Delany, Bryan Edwards, and Nathaniel Phillips were among the most recent Jamaican émigrés to join the long-established absentee families such as the Longs, Beckfords, and Pennants. They created a close-knit community in the metropole whose members lived up to the Jamaicans' reputation for excess.... But this select group of planters did more than enjoy their slave-based wealth; they spent a great deal of time minding their business. They gathered to discuss markets, trade, and colonial policy and were diligent in promoting their industry by participating in parliamentary politics. Most important, however, was the leadership role they played in 'the Society', which proved to be one of Britain's most powerful lobbies and achieved remarkable success in defending the interest of Jamaican and other West Indian planters.

David B. Ryden has extracted valuable information from the Minutes of the Society's meetings between May 1785 and May 1807 regarding, among other things, the most frequent attendees at these meetings. Overwhelmingly, the planter-merchants were associated with Jamaica. Of the fifty most frequent attendees at the Society's meetings in this period, thirty-nine were connected with Jamaica. Noteworthy, one of them, Beeston Long (Jr.), was Governor of the Bank of England between

1806 and 1808; he was also Chairman of the West India Merchants and the leading figure in the firm of merchants, Long, Drake and Long of 17 Bishopsgate, London. Edmund Pusey Lyon and Gibbs Walker Jordan were frequent attendees linked to Barbados; Lyon also had ties with Jamaica. The frequent attendees with connections to St. Vincent were James and George Baillie and William Manning; Grenada, St. Kitts and Demerara shared the Baillies; James Baillie was member of the British Parliament between 1792 and 1793. William Manning was shared with St. Kitts and the Danish West Indies; Manning was the agent for St. Vincent between 1792 and 1810; he was the head of the firm of merchants, William Manning, of 15 St. Mary, London.

Professor Ryden also compiled a summary list of the frequency distribution of the Society's Chairmanship between May 1785 and May 1807. Of the 27 Chairs of the Society in that period, only four were not listed as connected to Jamaica: John Brathewaite and Edmund Pusey Lyon linked to Barbados; William Knox was tied to Dominica; and Sir William Young had a nexus to St. Vincent, Antigua, and Tobago. Lord Richard Penrhyn held the Chairmanship most frequently, by far.

Still, holding the Chairmanship most frequently did not necessarily mean that the person was the most influential among the planter-merchant class. The Chairmanship was an important measure of influence or clout but not the only one. Take the case of Simon Taylor, one of the richest sugar barons, who attended only six meetings of the society in the early 1790s, and was Chairman only twice, due to fact that he was resident almost exclusively in Jamaica. Professor Ryden provides us with a summary profile of Simon Taylor, a cantankerous grandee:

> Despite the distance, Taylor took a keen interest in metropolitan and island politics while serving as a Jamaican Assemblyman for Kingston and for the parish of St. Thomas in the east. Perhaps more than any colonial, Simon Taylor coordinated political action in the Caribbean with that of the Society. The Jamaican Governor's wife, Maria Nugent, commented that Taylor was 'by much the richest proprietor in the island, and in the habit of accumulating [so much] money, so as to make his (heir and) nephew (Sir Simon Richard Brisset Taylor)...one of the most wealthy subjects of Her Majesty'. Taylor's wealth was matched

by political power in the island, for he had "great influence in the Assembly" despite being "nearly superannuated".... This bachelor lived the prototypical planter's life, "principally with overseers of estates and masters of merchant vessels". Taylor was immersed in planter politics, showing little patience for other pursuits and rejecting the 'society of (white) women'.

Indeed, Taylors' chairmanship of the Society on two occasions was an honour bestowed upon him when he was temporarily in London.

The most politically connected agent for the planter-merchant class was Sir William Young, who was not simply a lobbyist but was directly involved in governmental affairs as a member of Parliament for St. Mawes for 22 years between 1784 and 1806. His family had financial interests in St. Vincent, Antigua, and Tobago, and he inherited his father's four sugar estates in 1788. In the early 1790s he visited his plantations and recorded his observations in a published book entitled *A Tour through Several Islands of Barbados, St. Vincent, Tobago and Grenada in the Years 1791 and 1792*. Later he was appointed Governor of Tobago after demitting office as a member of Parliament for Buckingham borough (1806-1807). His 1793 marriage settlement with Barbara Talbot contained a 1792 enumeration of some 200 slaves on the St. Vincent Estate of Calliaqua. Young entered Parliament and was part of a circle of politicians that included William W. Grenville, the future Prime Minister who would coordinate, with William Wilberforce, the final passage of the Bill to abolish the slave trade in 1807. Young stood fervently for the West Indian planter-merchant interests in Parliament.

Hilary Beckles devotes an entire chapter of his book to the Earls of Harewood and their linkage to Queen Elizabeth II. He traces the evolution of the Lascelles family into the Harewoods, and then their ties with the British Royalty. Indeed, in 1966, Lord Harewood hosted the young Queen Elizabeth at his Belle Estate in Barbados, a sugar plantation which his family had owned since 1780. The Queen was in fact visiting her family's plantation, Lord Harewood being her first cousin. Commenting on this royal visit, Beckles tells it like it is:

It was the latest expression of the old partnership...sugar, slavery, and royalty... a 'merger' of slavery now consummated by marriage. In 1922, Viscount Lascelles, heir to the fifth Earl of Harewood, had married Princess Mary, the Princess Royal. As owner of the Belle estate in 1966, one of the many slave plantations that enriched the family, the seventh earl, George Lascelles, welcomed his first cousin... Her Majesty Queen Elizabeth II. Nothing was unusual about any of this. Barbados was the primary market for the enchained Africans supplied by the Royal African Company (formerly the Company of Royal Adventurers of England Trading with Africa), owned and administered by her ancestor, King James II.

The Harewood family's ten plantations in the West Indies were located in Barbados, Jamaica and Tobago. In Barbados there were four with an aggregate of 1,654 acres: Belle (year 1780-1975), Mount (1784-1974), Fortesque (1787–1918), and Thicketts (1787-1918); in Jamaica, there were three estates with an aggregate land acreage of 2,725 acres: Mammee Ridge in St. Ann (1777–1797), Nightingale Grove in St. Dorothy (1777-1836), and Willamsfield-in-the-Vale in St. Thomas (1777-1820). The other four estates were in Tobago: Richmond (1777-1820), Glamorgan (1777-1820), Goldsborough and Goodwood (1781-1818), an aggregate in Tobago of 2,326 acres. In all the plantation holdings of the Harewood family in the West Indies, at about the turn of the nineteenth century, amounted to 6,705 acres. On eight of these estates the principal activity was sugar cane cultivation and sugar production; one estate focussed on raising cattle; and another was mainly in cotton cultivation. On the Jamaican plantations alone, 1,250 enslaved Africans provided the labour power for the wealth accumulation of the Harewood family. The Belle Estate which Queen Elizabeth II visited in 1966 was acquired by the Lascelles (Harewoods) in 1780 with an enslaved population of 232.

In 1816, three of the Harewoods' estates — Thicketts, Fortescue and Mount — were sites for anti-slavery activity during "the war of General Bussa" in Barbados. The rebel army under "General" Bussa's command fought the militia and the imperial army at Thicketts plantation, inflicting massive damage upon the properties amounting, according to Beckles, in excess of £6 million in 2010 values.

The enslaved on Harewood's estates knew that the Earl of Harewood had campaigned against the abolition of the slave trade and that he was publicly a supporter of enslavement. Beckles informs us that the earl celebrated the crushing of Bussa's Rebellion and he openly commended Colonel Edward Cobb for spearheading the imperial troops which defeated the rebels. At a dinner in 1819 on Cobb's behalf, the earl contributed £200 (£139,000 in 2010) to Cobb's fund.

In the West Indies and England, the second Earl of Harewood continued to challenge the British anti-slavery movement. He was acknowledged on the eve of emancipation as an articulate and wealthy pro-slavery advocate. He was succeeded by his son, the third earl, who sat as a Member of Parliament for Northallerton. It was his great-grandson, the sixth earl, Henry George Charles Lascelles (1881-1947), who married Princess Mary, daughter of King George V. It was the seventh earl who entertained Her Majesty at Belle estate in 1966. Born in 1923, he died in July 2010, a generous contributor to music and English National Opera but with a historic wealth based on slavery and plantations in the West Indies.

Beckles details in his book the slave owners who sat in the British parliament and the entrepreneurs and financiers in the private sector who benefitted enormously from slavery. Drawing upon the impressive work done by Professor Nicholas Draper and his team at the University College of London, Beckles was able to piece together a despoiled tapestry of wealth accumulation by members of the ruling and governing classes in Britain, on the backs of the slaves. The descendants of these wealth accumulators are, in many cases, identifiable today. Beckles, for example, lists twenty-two British slave-owning Dukes, Marquesses, and Earls sourced from Nicholas Draper's book, *The Price of Emancipation: Slave-Ownership, Compensation and British Society at the End of Slavery* (Cambridge University Press, 2010). The details of these, and related disclosures, are a gold-mine to be tapped in the reparations cause. Three major British banks with historic enrichment from slavery are also identified: Barclays Bank, Lloyds Bank, and the Royal Bank of Scotland. So, too, are the two well-known merchant banking firms, Baring Brothers and the Rothschild banks which were, according to Beckles, "significant beneficiaries of their enterprises in the West Indies" and which "went to great lengths to defend slavery and to receive compensation cash for their slave investments."

Twenty Million Pounds: Slave Owners' Reparations

Professor Beckles commences his discussion on slave owners' reparations thus:

> In 1838, the British people ended their 250-year old 'national crime' of black enslavement with a sum total payment of £20 million to the last slave-owning cohort.... Slavery, then, came to an end with a festive orgy of public money being showered upon slave owners, who for generations had been financially enriched, socially elevated and celebrated, and politically empowered and protected. Their final pillage came in the form of massive financial reparations from the British treasury.

For the legally-freed enchained bodies, there was nothing. A certain future of immediate poverty and continued dispossession awaited them. Their socio-economic condition was one of continued underdevelopment. The text could be properly put thus: How Britain undeveloped the enchained Africans in the West Indies.

Robin Blackburn in his celebrated book, *The Overthrow of Colonial Slavery, 1776-1848* (Verso, 1988), informs us that:

> The size of the sum granted to the planters surprised even those who agreed to it. There was a fit of nervous hilarity when an MP pointed out, following the passage of the compensation clause, that the House usually haggled for hours before agreeing to the creation of a new post at a salary of £500 a year. At the close of the lengthy Cabinet session at which the precise compensation terms were hammered out the Prime Minister fell asleep where he sat; his colleagues tiptoed out in order not to wake him.... The slaves themselves were to cover a significant portion of the cost of the compensation since during the 'apprenticeship' period they were obliged to remain on the plantations and work a ten-hour day.

The data indicate that across sixteen slave colonies in the British West Indies, the slave-owners received an aggregate of £16,356,661 (£11.6 billion in 2010 values) for 655,780 slaves. These numbers are sourced by

Beckles from Nicholas Draper's *The Price of Emancipation*. The largest sums received were for slaves in Jamaica (£6.1 million); British Guiana (£4.28 million); Barbados (£1.7 million); and Trinidad (£1.02 million). The other twelve colonies from which the slave-owners received this compensation were: Anguilla, Antigua, Dominica, Grenada, British Honduras, Montserrat, Nevis, St. Kitts, St. Lucia, St. Vincent, Tobago and the Virgin Islands. The data were not provided for the Bahamas and Barbuda, unless the latter was included in the Antigua figure.

Slightly different figures are shown in other compilations of data. For example, the numbers for St. Vincent in Draper's book are 22,786 slaves and compensation of £570,300. The numbers which I have been using for St. Vincent are taken from Joseph Spinelli's 1973 doctoral dissertation *Land Use and Population in St. Vincent 1763–1960* which are: 22,997 slaves and a compensation of £592,509 or approximately £491.18 million or EC $2.05 billion in 2013 values. A factor of 839 has been authoritatively assessed to provide 2013 values of the 1838 numbers.

The slave-owners complained that they were paid roughly one-half of the valuation of their slaves. But they could not have been truly dissatisfied with their bounty from the British Treasury.

Nicholas Draper has suggested new ways to look at today's value of the £20 million compensation that the slave-owners received in 1838. Beckles quotes him thus from *The Price of Emancipation:*

> The British state of the 1830s was much smaller than it is today, and at 40 percent of government receipts or expenditures, £20 million was a huge amount; it would almost equate to £200 billion today.... Finally, in relation to the size of the economy, the £20 million compensation would be the equivalent of around £76 million.

Clearly, the quantification issues relating to reparations for slavery require further refinement and elaboration.

Beckles correctly advises that the slave owners won three decisive battles in securing reparations for their property rights in enslaved Africans. First, they received cash to refinance their business; in this regard, Beckles lists twenty-four British financiers who received reparations amounting to £594,339 (£423 million in 2010 values) for enslaved persons in Jamaica; the overall reparations figure for Jamaican slave-owners was £6.1 million (£4.3 billion in 2010 values or £5.12 billion in 2013 values) for 311,455 enslaved persons. Secondly, the slave-owners were able to make new investments, mostly in British stocks. And thirdly, the slave-owners succeeded in holding onto their West Indian enterprises and thereby rendering the "freed" persons largely landless, second-class citizens in the colonies where they were enslaved.

I leave the final words on this subject to Beckles' compelling and insightful prose:

> For the Caribbean, the plantation system remained. Blacks, now freed, entered into a period of intensive policing, racial apartheid and increased hostility to their demands for justice. The West Indies planters and merchants, and their London financiers, were pleased with the reparations deal. The blacks who had been the victims of the crime received nothing. This was the greatest crime of all committed by the British state against the African people.

The Case for Reparations: Challenges and Prospects

In Part II of Beckles' *Britain's Black Debt* there are four chapters which address for consideration a number of themes in going forward with a claim for reparations. The chapter headings speak for themselves:

> The Case for Reparations
> "Sold in Africa": The United Nations and Reparations in Durban
> British Policy: No Apology, No Reparations
> The Caribbean Reparations Movement

I shall conduct my review of this part of the book in an omnibus fashion.

The righting of historic wrongs is at the heart of the case for reparations for native genocide, lands "stolen", and slavery. It is grounded in justice and fairness. Professor Beckles draws our attention to an approach which the Permanent Court of International Justice (the predecessor of the International Court of Justice) in 1928 in the Chorzow Factory case between Germany and Poland. The Court held as follows:

> The essential principle contained in the actual notion of an illegal act is that reparation must, as far as possible, wipe out all the consequences of the illegal act and re-establish the situation which would, in all probability, have existed if that act had not been committed.

Beckles correctly identifies one of the central questions for the Caribbean reparations movement and any similar quest for compensation for historical and colonial crimes, as: What constitutes a meritorious claim?

In helping to answer this query Beckles turns to a learned article by Mari J. Matsuda entitled "Looking to the Bottom: Critical Legal Studies and Reparations", published in "Harvard Civil Rights – Civil Liberties Law Review", 22, no. 323, (1987). Matsuda suggests that a human injustice that attracts a claim of reparations must meet the following three criteria:

> The injustice must be well-documented; the historical data setting out the specifics of the injustice should withstand scientific scrutiny and be verifiable to the satisfaction of a court or tribunal.
>
> The victims must be identifiable as a distinct group.
>
> The current members of the group must continue to suffer harm.

Beckles is satisfied, and so am I, that the historical data on native genocide and slavery and on the contemporary condition of the descendants of those who suffered from the crimes against humanity are such as to make a proper fit for these three criteria. The awful legacy of native genocide and slavery is real; the terrible scars of underdevelopment are before our very eyes, sourced to native genocide and slavery. Beckles' *Britain's Black*

Debt is a major intellectual contribution in the practical struggle to lodge and successfully pursue a claim for reparations. But, as he admits, there is much more work to be done on all fronts to get there.

A bundle of legal arguments have been proffered by those who oppose reparations for native genocide and slavery. These revolve around doctrine of "relevant law and practice" at the time when the events giving rise to a claim of reparations, occurred; the idea of "remoteness"; the absence of the actual perpetrators of the crimes against humanity and the victims. Beckles advances answers to these propositions and I feel sure that appropriate and satisfactory legal responses to these possible challenges are available. Both international law and domestic British law provide persuasive answers. In any event, this is not only a legal battle but a moral, diplomatic, and political one, too, which has "reparations" and "settlement" on the continuum of options.

There is, too, the question of the proper forum to be utilised in making the claim for reparations. The possible options no doubt include: A complaint to the International Court of Justice (ICJ); a campaign to get the United Nations General Assembly (or other UN body) to seek an Advisory Opinion from the ICJ, pursuant to Article 65 of the Statute; a complaint to the relevant supervising United Nations Treaty bodies and/or Human Rights Council; a move to utilise the Commonwealth Secretariat as a mechanism for an agreement to launch an investigation into the requirement to provide reparations; possible Treaty-based claims arising from a bundle of bilateral and multilateral treaties; and domestic law proceedings in the United Kingdom Courts against the UK government, companies, institutions, and individuals.

Admittedly, there are some jurisdictional hurdles but they are not insurmountable. Possible, credible avenues thus exist to make the claim for reparations.

Then there are issues connected to quantification of the claim. Undoubtedly, there would be controversy over the factor or the multiplier to be used to bring historic values in line with present-day values. Professor Draper and his team at the University College of London, and others, have done sterling work in this area. One set of comparative measurements can be found in average wages across historical time; others may use, for example, comparators based on Gross Domestic Product (GDP) figures. Draper's analysis suggests, for instance, that the average wage values would deliver a factor of 839 between 1838 and 2013.

Then there is, too, the multiplicand or base to be used in the calculations. For example, do we use a base figure as "special damages" that which the slave-owners received in reparations in 1838 or a larger figure? Do we utilise Draper's innovative way of assessment in terms of the size comparatively of the slave-owners' compensation as a percentage of the size of the British economy?

Surely, too, there must be a sum quantified as general damages for pain, suffering, and loss endured by the "natives", slaves and their descendants, and the successor nation-states in the Caribbean in relation to native genocide, lands "stolen", forced deportation of natives, and slavery. Surely a claim for exemplary and aggravated damages must be in order. This is an area that requires further study and refinement, drawing also on the successful claims for reparations or settlement by the Jews and Maoris, for example.

Given the conceptual, moral and political, legal and historical justification for reparations, Hilary Beckles makes the powerful point that:

> Caribbean governments are well-placed to present a collective case on behalf of the descendant citizens of enslaved Africans and native peoples. These victims have a right to justice. Caribbean states have a moral and political obligation to their citizens that must be discharged in the interest of furthering legitimate democratic governance.

At the same time, it is important for us to recognise that "it is the intention of British society to walk away from these crimes without reparatory obligation and responsibility." As Beckles tells it the British state and society "do not intend to be held accountable." Thus, to this end:

> The state has made several arguments. As discursive positions they intend to deflect what officials understand to be a legally strong and morally compelling case that requires political

resolution before it reaches international courts formulated as crimes against humanity. That is, in framing these arguments, state officials understand them to be legally weak and morally unacceptable. The politics of opposition, therefore, is where the value of these arguments is to be found.

Let us be in no doubt that neo-colonialists, western European states, including Britain, international financial institutions, intelligence agencies from former colonial powers in the Caribbean schooled in the art of political chicanery, and more, will be put in the service of denying just reparation. They will all play it rough: intimidation, divide-and-rule, and subterfuge will be utilised against leaders and those Caribbean nation-states which are in the forefront of this monumental reparation cause. No sane person ought ever to forget that the former President of Haiti, Jean-Bertrand Aristide, was bundled out of office by the European-American axis shortly after he had formally submitted a claim to France for reparations for slavery in the sum of US $20 billion dollars. Immediately after his hand-picked, neo-colonial, successor, Gerard Latortue, entered the Haitian presidency he withdrew the reparations claim and denounced it as unachievable in his lifetime or at all; he opportunistically stated that he preferred to address the immediately pressing problems in Haiti of the economy, unemployment, and poor governance. He was hugely unsuccessful in tackling any of his preferences and left office as an outstanding failure, unheralded, unloved, and unimpressive. That fate awaits all opportunistic neo-colonials in our region.

In his book, Beckles explores the disappointments on the reparations issue at the United Nations World Conference against Racism, Discrimination, Xenophobia and Related Intolerance (WCAR) in Durban, South Africa, at the end of August 2001. The USA, Britain, and other Europeans countries, through their respective governments, threatened to walk out of the Conference if reparations was an agenda item. It was nevertheless discussed by them in an almost benign manner, more or less as an irritable side issue. Several African leaders danced around the subject to the rhythm, chords, and melody of the USA-Europe metaphoric orchestra and, at best, equivocated on this matter of enormous significance for the people of Africa and the Caribbean; some of the African leaders even accepted the neo-colonial lyrics. It was left to the contingents from the Caribbean, made up of delegates from a few governments and NGOs, to keep the fire burning on the reparations issue.

Fidel Castro, President of Cuba, and the only head of government from the Caribbean at the conference was the first to speak from the region. According to Beckles, Fidel "set the time and texture for a coherent diasporic response." Fidel was firm, committed, and clear in his views:

> Cuba speaks of reparations, and supports the idea as an unavoidable moral duty to the victims of racism, based on a major precedent, that is, the indemnification being paid to the descendants of the Hebrew people who in the very heart of Europe suffered the brutal and loathsome racist holocaust. However, it is not with the intent to undertake an impossible search for the direct descendants of the specific countries of the victims of actions which occurred throughout centuries.

> The irrefutable truth is that tens of millions of Africans were captured, sold like a commodity and sent beyond the Atlantic to work in slavery while seventy million indigenous people in the hemisphere perished as a result of European conquest and colonisation.

The final declaration of the Durban Conference contained a sting-in-the-tail against reparations. Among other things, it stated that:

> We acknowledge that slavery and the slave trade, including the transatlantic slave trade, were appalling tragedies in the history of humanity not only because of their abhorrent barbarism but also in terms of their magnitude, organised nature and especially their negation of the essence of the victims and further acknowledge that slavery and the slave trade are crimes against humanity and should always have been so.

This "should" caused the Caribbean delegations to stand formally against this and other equivocating paragraphs in the Declaration. Clearly, if the slave trade and slavery were not *always* crimes against humanity, the issue of reparations is thus placed in limbo or worse. At Durban, the CARICOM region had, among other persons, the Honourable Mia Mottley of the Barbados government and Hillary Beckles were formally authorised by me, as Prime Minister of St. Vincent and the Grenadines, to represent my country. There was a complete coincidence of views between the government of St. Vincent and the Grenadines and the Barbados delegation.

Beckles' discussion on the Durban Conference is an eye-opener to the unseemly compromise and even complete capitulation by several African countries and UN leaders, to the USA-European axis. So, too, is his discourse on "British Policy: No Apology, No Reparations." The New Labour Project of Tony Blair on this matter was disgraceful and indefensible; sadly, it drew into its orbit good and decent black members of Parliament and government ministers from the United Kingdom. They trotted out the old, worn-out, unsupportable arguments against reparations.

At the same time, in 2007, the voice of the Church of England, the Archbishop of Canterbury, Dr. Rowan Williams, was loud and clear on the side of justice for the descendants of slaves in the West Indies. In a sermon at Westminster Abbey (London, March 27, 2007) to mark the Bicentennial of the Abolition of the Slave Trade, the Archbishop aptly stated:

> We who are the heirs of the slave-owning and slave-trading nations of the past have to face the fact that our historic prosperity was built in large part on this atrocity; those who are the heirs of the communities ravaged by the slave trade know very well that much of their present suffering and struggling is the result of centuries of abuse.... Slavery is not a regional problem in the human world; it is hideously persistent in our nations and cultures. But today it is for us to face our history; the Atlantic trade was our contribution to this universal sinfulness.....
>
> Slavery was taken for granted by Christians and non-Christians and irreligious people for centuries if not millennia.... Yet the Spirit that spoke in Jesus was a Spirit contemporary and alive for

those who, two hundred years ago and more, refused to take it for granted because they saw something of the truth about God and about humanity.

Is that Spirit contemporary and alive in us today? If so, we shall have the courage to face the legacies of slavery.... We shall have the courage to turn to each other and ask how, together, we are to make each other more free and more human.

May the Spirit be upon us and in us in our struggles.

Across the Caribbean, especially after the bicentennial year (2007) of the abolition of the British transatlantic slave trade, the regional reparations movement, mirroring the global reparations struggles, "gained intensity in terms of recognition ceremonies, public education campaigns, and statements from political leaders."

At the United Nations' General Assembly several Caribbean leaders including Baldwin Spencer of Antigua and Barbuda, Dr. Denzil Douglas of St. Kitts and Nevis, Dame Billie Miller of Barbados, and Ralph E. Gonsalves of St. Vincent and the Grenadines formally placed the demand on record for reparations for slavery and native genocide.

In Jamaica, Barbados, Antigua and Barbuda, and St. Vincent and the Grenadines, Reparations Committees/Commissions have been established to pursue the matter with resoluteness. The Chairman of the St. Vincent and the Grenadines Reparations Committee is Jomo Thomas, a lawyer and anti-colonial and nationalist political activist.

A Note on Further Action

I advise briefly, in summary form, on further action, namely:

We must push for a CARICOM Commission on Reparations. This is urgent. It ought to be on the agenda for the Conference of Heads of State and Government in July 2013.

We must continue to advocate for reparations in all international fora. It must be a centre-piece of our region's foreign and domestic policies.

We must continue to educate our Caribbean people and our diaspora, and lift their awareness of the reparations issue. This must be a focused, huge, on-going educational campaign.

We must assemble a competent and committed body of experts (historians, economists, statisticians, lawyers, and other professionals) to prepare the case, including the sums of money and other initiatives in areas such as the economy, education, health, housing, poverty reduction, infrastructural development, technology transfer, rural transformation, air and sea transportation, and culture and tangible memorials, required as reparations.

We must establish links with other populations who seek or have sought reparations including the Maoris, the descendants of African slaves internationally, indigenous populations globally, Jews and Palestinians.

A CARICOM push for reparations must include the very special case of Haiti, a country which was coerced into paying France reparations for securing its very freedom and independence. Haiti paid reparations to France from 1825 to 1922 but the final portion of the debt in that year was paid by a loan from the USA which was only repaid completely in 1947. (Randall Robinson tells the gripping story factually and well in his book *An Unbroken Agony: Haiti, From Revolution to the Kidnapping of a President* (Basic Civitas Books, 2007.)

A special regional Conference on reparations, including governments, NGOs and distinguished personalities of relevance ought to be convened. St. Vincent and the Grenadines is prepared to host it.

A Final Appeal

I appeal to all right-thinking persons in the Caribbean, Britain, Africa, the Americas, and the entire world to embrace reparations for slavery and native genocide as just. The case for reparations is unanswerably strong. Those who have been opposed or indifferent to reparations, I urge you to rethink the matter, search your soul, and identify with the claim for appropriate recompense. The rethinking and soul-searching of the eighteenth century British slave-trading sea captain John Newton, who came to a full understanding of the unspeakable and unacceptable crime of slavery on his way to his calling as a preacher of the Gospel, is apt in the circumstances. In 1772, he penned the hymn "Amazing Grace" which has moved generations of hardened skeptics, cynics, and wayward souls, particularly its first verse:

> Amazing grace! (how sweet the sound!)
> That saved a wretch like me!
> I once was lost, but now am found
> Was blind, but now I see.

IV.
Road Map for Reparations for Native Genocide and Slavery in the Caribbean

Address to the Opening of the Regional Conference on Reparations for Native Genocide and Slavery at Victoria Park, St. Vincent and the Grenadines, on Sunday, September 15, 2013.

First, I welcome you my brothers, sisters, comrades from across the Caribbean, and globally, to St. Vincent and the Grenadines, a magnificent component of our unique and noble Caribbean civilisation, a bastion of regional integration and solidarity, and a strengthening, and committed, column in the national, regional, and international struggle against colonialism, imperialism, racism, and zenophobia. St. Vincent and the Grenadines stands for peace, justice, equality, liberty, and democracy; we hold dear the fundamental internationalist values of sovereignty and independence of peoples, and subscribe unequivocally to the central tenets of the Charter of the United Nations, grounded in multi-lateralism, not in a triumphalist, unilateralist push for hegemony. We are a small nation; one of the smallest in the world in terms of population, geographic size, and material resources. However, as a people, we recognise our humanity and thus our importance. We are not better than anyone else, but no one is better than us. We possess strengths and weaknesses, possibilities and limitations.

I know that I speak for the entire Caribbean when I affirm that it is our elemental duty to act in solidarity with each other, nationally and regionally, and in concert with our like-minded friends and allies internationally, in such a manner as to fortify our strengths, enhance our possibilities, cause our weaknesses and limitations to metamorphose into strengths and possibilities, and as far as is humanly possible, to reduce these weaknesses and limitations. These are our individual and collective duties and obligations in our quest to further ennoble our Caribbean civilisation in every material particular and to act in furtherance of our people's humanisation.

This nation, St. Vincent and the Grenadines, like all others in the Caribbean, has had an uneven record in its struggle for sovereignty, independence, individual and collective emancipation, and existential humanity. We have had successes and failures; triumphs and defeats. The forces of reaction, colonialism, and imperialism have not infrequently found the unpatriotic and opportunistic among us to be used, misused, and manipulated as "fifth-columnists" in their efforts to derail the march of humanity's progress and our people's upliftment. So, victories won have to be consolidated; and we must always be on guard to resist those who act, in whatever guise, contrary to the people's interest. And wherever there are setbacks, we must turn them into advances.

Much in our Vincentian history inspires us: the nobility and courage of Joseph Chatoyer, Chief of the Garifuna people; the heroism and sacrifices of the Garifuna people in the face of an extensive genocidal campaign perpetrated against them by the British; the resoluteness, dignity, and comradeship in struggle and suffering of our African ancestors who endured slavery; the solidity and ambition of our indentured forbears from Madeira and India; the increasing commitment to our Caribbean nationhood of more recent arrivants to our shores; and the steadfastness to, and adaptation of, our nation's ideals by those patriotic descendants of the Anglo-Saxon predecessors who had earlier participated ignobly in conquest and settlement.

Our Caribbean civilisation has been moulded from, and by, the indigenous population and peoples of disparate lands and places, in the landscape and seascape of the Caribbean. In the process, the oppression and suffering of the Kalinago, the Garifuna, and enchained Africans, have been rightly adjudged to have been a horrendous crime against humanity. Accordingly, the collective voice of our Caribbean civilisation ought justly to ring out for reparations for native genocide and African slavery from the successor states of the European countries which committed organised state-sponsored native genocide and African enslavement. The awful legacy of these crimes against humanity...a legacy exists today in our Caribbean, ought to be repaired for the developmental benefit of our Caribbean societies and all our peoples. The historic wrongs of native genocide and African slavery, and their continuing contemporary consequences, must be righted, must be repaired, in the interest of our people's humanisation. The European nations must partner in a focussed, especial way with us to execute this repairing. Thus, the demand for reparations is the responsibility not only of the descendants, in today's Caribbean, of the Kalinago, the Garifuna, the Amerindian, and the African. It is undoubtedly an agenda for all of us to advance, to promote, to concretise, and to execute. And the European nations which engaged in conquest, settlement, genocide, and slavery in our Caribbean must provide the reparatory resources required to repair the contemporary legacy of their historic wrongs. This repairing of the mind, of collective memory, of our economies, of our societies is part and parcel of the rebirth, the redemption, the further ennoblement of our Caribbean, our indigenous populations, our African descendants, and indeed of Africa.

Undoubtedly, the descendants of the Kalinago, the Garifuna, the Amerindians, and the Africans have an especial obligation to fight for reparatory justice. After all, their forbears were directly affected and, most importantly, together, they constitute the majority population across our Caribbean. Clearly, too, the struggle for, and leadership within, the national and regional reparations movement is for persons of every class, creed, race or ethnic group. We are all in it together. That is the nature of our Caribbean civilisation. And our entire civilisation stands to benefit from reparatory justice; it is not about payment of monies to individuals. It is a collective enterprise of our Caribbean civilisation.

I am urging that all Caribbean people, at home and abroad, to come aboard the reparations train and participate meaningfully in its journey for reparatory justice. This issue is huge; it is a fundamental, defining matter of our age and for this 21st century. It is a great cause, and great causes have never been won by doubtful men and women. "Reparations" is a subject which no one ought to trivialise. For example, there are those who demand that "reparations" be first made to Tom, Dick, Mary, or Jane who consider that this or that Caribbean government or leader has wronged them. Remedies for such wrongs are available in the national legal and political systems. If one uses the concept of "reparations" loosely, for anything and everything, it loses its real meaning for us.

It has been established in international law that "reparation must, as far as possible, wipe out all the consequences of the illegal act and re-establish the situation which would, in all probability, have existed if that act had not been committed". A claim for reparations revolves, critically, around three criteria: the injustice or historic wrong in question must be well-documented; the victims of the injustice or historic wrong must be identifiable as a distinct group; and the current members of the group must continue to suffer the consequences of this injustice or wrong. In our Caribbean, the case for reparations for native genocide and slavery is surely unanswerable.

Although European governments have been steadfast against reparations, some voices of reason, faith, and conscience have been heard in some important quarters in Europe in support of reparations. One such voice has been that of the former Archbishop of Canterbury, Dr. Rowan Williams who argued cogently on this subject on the side of justice for the descendants of slaves in the West Indies. In a sermon at Westminster Abbey (London, May 27, 2007) to mark the Bicentennial of the Abolition of the Slave Trade, Archbishop Williams stated:

> We who are the heirs of the slave-owning and slave-trading nations of the past have to face the fact that our historic prosperity was built in large part on this atrocity; those who are the heirs of the communities ravaged by the slave trade know very well that much of their present suffering and struggling is the result of centuries of abuse.... Slavery is not a regional problem in the human world; it is hideously persistent in our nations and cultures. But today, it is for us to face our history; the Atlantic trade was our contribution to this universal sinfulness....

Slavery was taken for granted by Christians and non-Christians and irreligious people for centuries if not millennia.... Yet the spirit that spoke in Jesus was a Spirit contemporary and alive for those who, two hundred years ago and more, refused to take it for granted because they saw something of the truth about God and humanity.

Is that Spirit contemporary and alive in us today? If so, we shall have the courage to face the legacies of slavery.... We shall have the courage to turn to each other and ask how together, we are to make each other more free and more human.

May the Spirit be upon us and in us in our struggles.

As a mode of proceeding, I advise, too, that we make every effort to build solidarity ties with like-minded persons and groups overseas, including in Europe. We must strive to build support across national and ethnic lines. Our CARICOM governments will have to engage, formally, the governments of Britain, France, and Holland — the former colonial powers which designed and executed the historic wrongs and injustices against the native populations and enslaved Africans. Further, it is necessary and desirable to interface in a structured manner with our brothers and sisters in Africa, including their governments; the African-Caribbean nexus is vital. This quest for reparations is a global project of extraordinary proportions and must be addressed accordingly. I thus expect that each government of the CARICOM member-states will cause to be inserted a strong, positive message on reparations in the speech of its Head of State, Head of Government or Foreign Minister, who addresses the United Nations General Assembly next week. I certainly will be doing so on behalf of St. Vincent and the Grenadines.

On Tuesday, September 17th, I will be in Trinidad to attend a meeting of the Bureau of the Heads of Government Conference of CARICOM under the current chairmanship of the distinguished Prime Minister of Trinidad and Tobago, my dear sister Kamla Persad-Bissessar. Among the issues to be canvassed relates to the status of the reparations project.

Last week I was in Guyana at the CARICOM Headquarters where I held extensive discussions with CARICOM's Secretary General and his senior staff on the priority agenda items for CARICOM under my Chairmanship which will commence on January 01, 2014. The quest for reparations is among the central priorities.

It will be noted that at this Regional Conference on Reparations there are representatives from every member-state of CARICOM, representatives from supportive organisations, from Europe and North America, including representatives from the Garifuna in the USA, and representatives from the Cuban government. I am so happy to see everyone. Cuba's solidarity is particularly instructive, and flows inexorably from its well-established, selfless internationalism and its clear grasp of the reparations issue. In August 2001, in Durban, South Africa, at the United Nations World Conference Against Racism, Discrimination, Xenophobia and Related Intolerance (WCAR), Fidel Castro was unequivocal on the matter when he outlined that:

> Cuba speaks of reparations, and supports the idea as an unavoidable moral duty to the victims of racism based on major precedent, that is, the indemnification being paid to the descendants of the Hebrew people who in the very heart of Europe suffered the brutal and loathsome racist holocaust. However, it is not with the intent to undertake an impossible search for the direct descendants of the specific countries of the victims of actions which occurred throughout centuries.
>
> The irrefutable truth is that tens of millions of Africans were captured, sold like a commodity and sent beyond the Atlantic to work in slavery while seventy million indigenous people in the hemisphere perished as a result of European conquest and colonisation.

On May 02, 2013, in Kingston, Jamaica, at the formal launch of Hilary Beckles' book, *Britain's Black Debt: Reparations for Caribbean Slavery and Native Genocide*, I ended my presentation as the book reviewer with a seven-point summary for immediate action, at the minimum. Three of the seven items have been successfully addressed, namely (i) the decision of CARICOM Heads to establish a CARICOM Commission on Reparations;

(ii) the inclusion of Haiti as a very special case for the reparations struggle; and (iii) the convening of a special regional conference on reparations in St. Vincent and the Grenadines.

Four items on the immediate agenda, which I advanced, remain to be pursued:

The continued advocacy for reparations in all international fora. This issue must be a center-piece of our region's foreign and domestic policies.

The continued education of our Caribbean people and lifting of their awareness of the reparations issue. This must be a focussed, huge, on-going educational campaign.

The establishment of structured links with other populations who seek or have sought reparations including the Maoris, the descendants of African slaves internationally, indigenous populations globally, Jews and Palestinians.

The assembling of a competent and committed body of experts (historians, economists, statisticians, lawyers, and other professionals) to prepare the case, including the sums of money and other initiatives required as reparations in areas such as the economy, education, health, housing, poverty reduction, infrastructure development, technology transfer, rural transformation, air and sea transport, and culture and tangible memorials. There is a lot of preparatory, detailed work to be done to carry forward the political, diplomatic, and legal struggle. This is urgent.

The extent of the material resources to be demanded as reparations must of necessity bear a close relationship to what was illegally or wrongly extracted and exploited (land, wealth, people), from the Caribbean by the European colonialists, including the compensation paid to the slave owners at the time of the abolition of slavery. But the repairing has to do with the contemporary legacy or consequences of native genocide and slavery. It is this continuing contemporary legacy or consequential condition which provides the historical nexus, philosophical frame, and factual base for the political, diplomatic, and legal case for reparatory justice.

I agree entirely with Hilary Beckles' stance in his recent book, *Britain's Black Debt* that the quest for reparations is not an anti-Britain crusade on account of Britain's central role in the crimes of native genocide and slavery in the Caribbean. This quest for reparatory justice is not a confrontational exercise though we must make the case for reparations as robustly as the circumstances demand. It is worth quoting Beckles on this:

> The Caribbean reparation case against Britain is not based on any concept or intention to participate in political confrontation with the British society or its government. A confrontational approach to reparation does not hold reconciliation as a primary objective. Reconciliation, however, is the necessary outcome of the claim for reparations, seeking as it does to establish a spirit of mutual respect and obligation between the British state and the descendants of enslaved Africans who continued to be victimised a century after legislative emancipation in 1838.
>
> ...It is important for British society to acknowledge that its development as a nation-state, the transformation of its economy to sustainable industrialisation, and its global standing as a super power among nations were founded upon a crime against humanity in a form of racial chattel enslavement of African bodies and the global trafficking of millions of those bodies for three hundred years.
>
> Acknowledging and accounting for wrongs is deeply enshrined in British law and society. And as such, the need to engage British society with a reparations discourse is consistent with national, cultural, and intellectual norms. Indeed, the British intellectual and moral traditions should insist upon it. Far from seeing reparations claims as confrontational, then, British society, should champion the cause as an expression of respect and of celebration of the finest aspects of its judicial culture.

What is being said here of Britain in relation to its former British colonial possessions in the Caribbean, can with more or less equal force be said of France as regards Haiti, and of Holland in respect to Suriname!

I appeal to all right-thinking persons in the Caribbean, Britain, France, Holland, the European Union, Africa, the Americas, and the entire world to embrace reparations for native genocide and slavery as just. The case for reparations, I reiterate, is unanswerably strong. Those who have been opposed or indifferent to reparations, I urge you to rethink the matter, search your souls, and identify with the claim for appropriate recompense. The rethinking and soul-searching of the 18th century British slave-trading sea captain John Newton, who came to a full understanding of the unspeakable and unacceptable crime of slavery on the way to his calling as a preacher of the Gospel, is apt in the circumstances. In 1772, he penned the hymn "Amazing Grace" which has moved generations of hardened skeptics, cynics, and wayward souls, particularly its first verse:

> Amazing grace, how sweet the sound!
> That saves a wretch like me!
> I once was lost, but now am found
> Was blind, but now I see!

Made in the USA
Columbia, SC
30 September 2020